GUARDIANS OF HOPE

The Angels' Guide to Personal Growth

Books by Terry Lynn Taylor

Messengers of Light:
The Angels' Guide to Spiritual Growth

Guardians of Hope:
The Angels' Guide to Personal Growth

Answers From the Angels:
A Book of Angel Letters

Creating With the Angels:
An Angel-Guided Journey Into Creativity

GUARDIANS OF HOPE

The Angels' Guide to Personal Growth

Terry Lynn Taylor

H J Kramer Inc
Tiburon, California

Published by H J Kramer Inc
P.O. Box 1082
Tiburon, CA 94920

Editor: Nancy Grimley Carleton
Illustrations: Marty Noble
Cover Art: Adolphe-William Bouguereau,
   La Vierde aux Anges (detail)
Cover Design: Spectra Media
Composition: Classic Typography
Book Production: Schuettge & Carleton
Bouguereau Painting:
   Courtesy of Musée du Petit-Palace, Paris,
   Giraudon/Art Resource, New York
Manufactured in the United States of America
10 9 8 7 6 5 4

Library of Congress Cataloging-in-Publication Data:

Taylor, Terry Lynn, 1955–
    Guardians of hope : the angels' guide to personal growth / Terry
Lynn Taylor.
       p.   cm.
    Includes bibliographical references.
    ISBN 0–915811–52–9 : $9.95
    1. Angels.   2. Self-actualization (Psychology) — Religious aspects.
3. Spiritual life.   I. Title.
BL477.T38   1992
291.2'15 — dc20   91–53234
                                                              CIP

This book is dedicated to my parents, Gordon and Nancy Taylor. The older I get, the more I realize how blessed I was by the unconditional love they gave me in my childhood.

T.L.T.

To Our Readers

The books we publish are our contribution to an emerging world based on cooperation rather than on competition, on affirmation of the human spirit rather than on self-doubt, and on the certainty that all humanity is connected. Our goal is to touch as many lives as possible with a message of hope for a better world.

Hal and Linda Kramer, Publishers

Contents

Foreword

I generally think of my friend Terry Lynn Taylor in an aura of peace, joy, and mystery. Peace, because there's a sense of well-being when you are with her. Joy, because her very being exudes happiness and mystery, because there is that otherworldly feeling about her. The first time I saw her, I was attending a large book convention. Her publisher introduced us to each other, and at that moment I thought to myself, "Here's a kindred spirit in her wanderings through the universe."

From that meeting onward, Terry and I have maintained a beautiful communication. Even though we've only been together in the physical realm for limited periods of time, we have kept in touch through thoughts, dreams, or the more normal channel of the telephone.

When we met, Terry gave me an autographed coy of her first book on angels, *Messengers of Light*. I am a voracious reader and will normally read twenty books to find one good one. After completing *Messengers of Light*, I found it so good that I placed it in my special library with such classics as Richard Bach's *Illusions* and Dan Millman's *Way of the Peaceful Warrior*.

Terry's writing was so simple and beautiful that I found myself hoping that she would write another book about angels. And, now, here is her new book, *Guardians of Hope*. Her readers will enjoy the pragmatic aspect of her work. Terry blends esoteric knowledge and historical information with experiences from her own life to give us extremely practical insights into the world of angels. As you read, you will find yourself waxing philosophical at times. Then there will be other instances where you will want to underline every sentence in a chapter. The end result is a heightened awareness of the infinite potential of the human soul.

For those who feel that life seems dark and dreary, this book, together with Terry's earlier book, will bring you hope and comfort. You will understand that you are not alone in this vast universe but that you are surrounded by beings of light who are not only willing but anxious to assist you. All you have to do is ask, then be receptive to the answer.

I am grateful to Terry for having written such a useful book. I am even more grateful that she is my friend and that she shares her wisdom unselfishly with all. It is my hope that she will continue to write, and I look forward with anticipation to her future books. Thank you, Terry, and thanks to the guardians of hope.

John Harricharan
Author of *When You Can Walk
on Water Take the Boat* and
Morning Has Been All Night Coming

Special Thanks

Gratitude is not always easy to express on paper; there is something missing — perhaps a hug or warm smile. However, I would like to extend my thanks and angel blessings to the following people.

First of all, I would like to thank Nancy Grimley Carleton, MFCC, of Berkeley, California, the editor of this book. She is a great "book therapist," in addition to her professional practice as a psychotherapist. I knew all along she would be the editor of this book, and knowing this set me free to "just write."

Hal and Linda Kramer truly understand the nature of people and creativity. I thank them for offering me another chance to share angels with the world and for their flexibility and wisdom. Linda Kramer spent many hours reading through earlier versions of the manuscript and coached me through some not-so-creative times, always leaving me with a positive sense of inspiration. I thank Linda's friend, Nancy Gardner, who offered valuable feedback on an early draft. My thanks also goes to Hal and Linda's assistant, Uma Ergil, for always being there unconditionally.

I thank Jan Shelley for the time she spent reading through the earlier manuscripts. Many parts of the book would not have bloomed without Jan's insight and sharing.

I thank the angels for my special friendship with John Harricharan. He has been such a positive force in my life, and I feel highly honored that he took the time to write the foreword for this book.

I thank my nieces Elizabeth Ann Godfrey and Jessica Marie Godfrey for their contributions to the book and for the inspiration and humor they relay straight from the angels.

I would also like to thank Ken Cousens for permission to quote one of his wonderful poems.

This book was also influenced by my closest friends; they gave feedback on the book and were always there for me, just like the angels. I thank the following friends from the brightest light in my heart (in no particular order): Shannon Boomer, Linda Hayden, Jai Italiander, and Mary Beth Crain.

I also thank every member of my immediate family; they taught me at a young age the priceless value of unconditional love by action and example. I especially thank my parents, Nancy and Gordon, for helping me through the less prosperous days in the life of this book.

Introduction:

Opening Comments on Angels

You and I have a special gift we were endowed with having been born human. We have the ability to make choices. We can choose to see the world however we want to see it, regardless of our circumstances. This book is about using this special gift to our utmost advantage, by making positive choices that have favorable outcomes. Making positive choices is not always easy, because of the negative patterns and habits we have adopted. *Guardians of Hope* will guide you in contacting the angels who can help you make the choices that best serve your personal and spiritual growth.

One very special source of guidance is our guardian angel. Our guardian angel, as well as other angels, is available to help us make positive choices that bring us inner happiness not dependent on external factors. Our guardian angel will help us uncover the special gifts we were born with, such as intuition, creativity, and serenity. As we uncover our special gifts, the angels will help us find a path where we can express ourselves freely.

Since writing my first book on angels, *Messengers of Light,* I have personally used the "angel practices" you will find in the following chapters; these exercises have helped serenity flourish in my life.

To set the tone of *Guardians of Hope,* I first want to offer some opening comments on angels to enable you to jump right into the water of this book and know which way the tide is going.

What Are Angels?

Angels are messengers of light from heaven, the divine providence. The English language acquired the word *angel* from the Greek word *angelos,* meaning messenger, which was a translation of the Hebrew word for messenger, *mal'ak.* Angels relay messages from a higher spiritual power. They are divine beings; they are not of the social world or the physical earth. When you attract angels into your life, you are attracting the divine — you are connecting with the realm of heaven.

Angels are always available to help you create heaven in your life. There are angels for every occasion, including personal angels, such as guardians, spiritual guides, cheerleaders, and soul angels, who are always with us; angels of the moment, such as healers, miracle engineers, and rescuers; angels who embellish human life, such as worry extinguishers, fun executives, and prosperity brokers; nature devas, who watch over and help Mother Nature; and even designer angels, who can help with almost any task you assign. Angels' primary concern is to help transform human attitudes toward the positive, lighter side of life.

Angels enrich our thinking by instilling noble thoughts and ideas. They help us understand our higher nature and cleanse our imagination, allowing us a direct line to heaven. If we allow it, angels rescue us from danger, hopelessness, and despair. They can lift our spirits and teach us to find divine humor in all our experiences. Angels promote beauty, peace, and joy on the earth and offer it to anyone free for the taking. Angels also occasionally pose as humans for our benefit.

Angels are not extraterrestrials, earthbound spirits, or disembodied spirits someone can channel. They are not fairies or ghosts. Angels are not self-serving, prejudiced, or judgmental in any way toward human beings. Angels never interfere with our free will or create a negative situation. Angels never hurt us or instill fear with their presence.

Believing in Angels

A belief in angels is not exclusive to a particular religion. Most of the world's religions include a belief in angels, but you do not have to believe in a religion to enjoy the benefits of angels. However, angels *are* employed by a higher power, meaning God. Angels do not care what name you give to God, or what gender you assign to God; the basic common denominator they respond to is simply that *God is love.*

I do not like to debate the existence of angels. The way I see it, either you believe in angels or you don't; either way, I respect your opinion. I go a step beyond belief. I don't *believe in* angels; I *know* them. I know they exist in my life; they are a large part of the reality I have created for myself, and I must say I am glad I did. Too often when we say we believe something, someone comes along and asks us to prove it. Usually they want proof in a visual form, something they can see and possibly touch. It is difficult to prove the existence of angels to someone stuck in the seeing-is-believing mode. I am going to ask you to set aside the seeing-is-believing mind-set; don't even waste your energy on believing in angels for the sake of this book. Have you ever actually seen a radio wave? A radio station can send a sound many miles through the air without wires, and if we have the right type of receiver turned on, we will hear it. This might seem like magic to a person who knows nothing of radios. In the case of angels, we are the receivers, and even though we don't often get the chance to see them, angels are here all around us, just like radio and television signals.

I often picture life as offering us a choice of movie theaters with various movies playing. It is so rewarding to be in the right movie theater—the one where the angels are showing the movie representing God's unconditional love, available to all of us at no charge. This theater is always open, and the tickets are free and scattered everywhere; just pick one up and walk right in.

Are There Bad Angels?

Many people ask me about fallen angels, or demons. I personally believe that for every positive aspect of life, there is an opposite, negative aspect. Since angels are purely positive in nature, they have a counterpart we call demons, who are only negative in nature. It helps to visualize angels as pure light, not necessarily having any other form, such as bodies with wings and so forth. Then we can think of demons not as little devilish, ugly creatures but as pure darkness, "black space," if you will. Picture a totally dark room full of black space. In your imagination, open the door and with a small beacon of light, say a flashlight, begin to shine light around the room. The light transforms the darkness, illuminating the space so you can see what's there. Let's say that this darkness is full of demons, and they must run away from the light and hide from it. Now you turn on a light that lights the whole room; where are the demons going to go? They cannot exist in the light, so they must leave.

Now let's picture angels and demons as forms or beings. Angels are usually portrayed as tall beings and demons as very small, creepy-looking animal-type beings. Now think about what happens when demons are pursuing us and angels step in front of them: The demons are blinded by the tall beam of light and hide. Of course, all of this is actually much more complicated, but one element stands out in favor of each side. On the angels' side, the element is love, the one thing demons don't understand and don't have. On the demons' side, the element is fear, which is what demons thrive on and something angels never use. If we are fearful of the dark, of the world, of life, demons can gain power from us and play tricks on us to make us even more fearful. To change this scenario, we must become fearless and loving and call on the angels to create a barrier to the demons. This is the same as surrounding ourselves with white light. Remember: The light not only protects us; it transforms the darkness.

There may well be fallen angels, or, demons, who attack the good in people. But remember that anything you give attention to becomes powerful in your life. So why give power to believing in and concerning yourself with demons and fallen angels? Become part of the light yourself; the more light we humans generate, the less space the demons have to hide in! Another point to remember is that demons have no sense of humor and are usually attracted to humorless humans. So keep your sense of humor alive; the angels will be nearby, and the demons will make themselves scarce.

How Angels Make Their Presence Known

Angels have fun ways of letting us know they are around. They arrange coincidences and favorable meetings to get our attention. They also let us know they're with us by providing humor (attacks of hilarity and mirth) during serious events; giving us unexplainable feelings of peace and well-being during trying times; surrounding us with "good luck" and fortunate situations; leaving an exquisite scent in the air resembling roses or jasmine, which may intoxicate our minds for a moment; helping feelings of true hope and optimism glow in our hearts; and providing peak experiences of joy and love that sometimes rush through us.

Angels Are Always With Us

When we first develop angel consciousness, all sorts of wonderful synchronisms and charm-filled experiences come our way. As with anything, however, such as listening to our favorite song too many times, it becomes time to move to the next stage, to find a new favorite song. When it is time to progress, we may have to deal with an uncomfortable experience, sometimes called by spiritual seekers "the dark night of the soul."

Some people start their spiritual search when they begin to feel that there must be something more to life than the material gratification of wealth and earthly pursuits. The quest for something more starts when a nagging sense of boredom with life sets in. The quest usually leads to the idea that a higher power can fulfill empty feelings of boredom deep in one's soul. And the seeker finds that this is the truth. But it does not end there.

A few things happen after the initial step onto the spiritual path. First, the traveler needs courage and perseverance because old maps and well-trodden routes won't work anymore. Traveling a spiritual path entails charting new courses of thought patterns and changing habits that interfere with spiritual growth. Second, after the initial spiritual "peak experiences" may come a period of true spiritual battle. In his book *Chop Wood, Carry Water*, Rick Fields explains this well: "The initial euphoria that comes through the first awakening into even a little consciousness, except in a very few cases, will pass away . . . leaving a sense of loss, or feeling of falling out of grace, or despair. *The Dark Night of the Soul*, by St. John of the Cross, deals with that state."

The dark night of the soul is by no means an easy time, but it does not mean you have fallen out of grace, and it doesn't have to involve prolonged periods of despair. In fact, the dark night of your soul could be simply one difficult night or hour when you suffered spiritually, then were delivered back into the light rather quickly. So, please, don't make this more difficult than it has to be. Many of us enjoy drama, and I have seen some people so carried away with their own dark night of the soul that you would think the angels have an academy award ceremony once a year in heaven and these people want to be in the running. If you are going through a dark night of the soul, please allow the angels to illuminate the dark for you; do this by asking them to guide you safely to the dawn.

Angels do not abandon us, but it feels that way sometimes if we begin to be dependent on their magical ways and forget our part of the work, or play. If things are not going our way, we mostly have ourselves to blame. So, for heaven's sake, don't blame the angels or think they have abandoned you. They are right there waiting for you to take yourself less seriously so they can continue to guide you upward. One theme of this book is discovering ways to use help *not* offered on the earth, but offered in the kingdom of heaven for life on earth. We do this by bringing the emissaries of heaven, the angels, into our lives as spiritual business partners and friends. The angels are always with us.

Cocreating Life

One of the main spiritual realizations that has set me free is the knowledge that God is a cocreator. Cocreation implies a team effort. We are the human part of God's cocreative ability. Together with God and the angels, we cocreate our destinies. Having this realization changed my whole outlook on life. Instead of thinking about God as a parental figure, an object of my demands, a force that could give me what I wanted if the conditions were proper, I came to see my role as God's partner in creating the things I want.

The angels helped me arrive at this realization. When I request something from the angels (God), I know they will be "playing" with me to make it come about. In other words, I must look for the clues and opportunities here on earth to make my dreams and wishes come true. When you ask God and the angels to join you in creating your destiny, the light of love shines down on your path and an unimaginable feeling of grace begins to expand into all areas of your life. Negative thoughts about being a victim vanish with angels in your life, because you discover (or recover) your cocreative power. Getting rid of any idea about

God being an oversized parent in the sky helps us realize we can't be punished for doing anything childish or silly. God is our partner, not our punisher. Knowing that we create our destinies in partnership with God and the angels may seem like a simple thought. Simple as it is, I feel that it is the key we are looking for but so often miss. That is, people talk about cocreating their destiny and they experiment with manifestation techniques, but until they internalize the idea that the other part of themselves is God and the angels, they will not truly reach full empowerment. Our energy is of equal importance in the process of cocreation.

So keep your spirituality simple. If you want something to happen in your life, ask God and the angels, then ask yourself to assist in its creation. Asking ourselves to make it happen keeps us in alignment with our highest goals and allows for change. When you ask God and the angels, simply ask. At one time in my life, I used to pray by begging. I would say, "Please, God, I really want such and such to happen." I found myself constantly pleading and begging. Now I simply have a dialogue with God and thank God for heavenly assistance, trusting that the highest good will be done. I assure you that there *is* magic in the universe, but it is up to us to cocreate it. God and the angels exist in the unseen realm of heaven; you exist in the physical realm of earth. Together, you can have the best of both worlds; attune yourself to the ways of your cocreators and you will know how to play the crazy game of life. Remember your seventh sense — your sense of humor — another shared aspect of your cocreation with God.

Happiness

You may be reading this book because you are interested in the fun and excitement angels provide in the lives of humans, and perhaps you want more of it. You may *know* angels exist because they have proved it by saving you or a loved one from imminent danger or hopelessness. You may also be a person who deep inside wants to be happy and knows angels can be very helpful in the pursuit of true happiness—not happiness based outside yourself, but rather happiness from within.

Happiness is not just a fairy tale, and it is not reserved for a chosen few. There really are ways to live happily on this planet. There really are happy people on this planet. There really are happy conditions on this planet. The opposite is also true; unfortunately, the opposite may in fact be the norm for most of the planet—unnecessarily. In this book, I focus on the light side of the spectrum, by exploring practices and formulas that lead to happiness that blossoms and grows, allowing you to find a comfortable home within your soul and spirit.

Personal happiness is a noble quest. It is crucial for world happiness. I am talking here about happiness without reason. This type of happiness is actually a state of mind, or a state of grace. It has nothing to do with the conditions of your life or what possessions you have. It comes from a deep sense of your own self-worth and a respect for life. Happiness without reason gives you an ease of being in the world, a sense of belonging.

Angels are our role models for happiness. Angels are happiness trainers, and they want the very best for each of us. Angels are our cheerleaders. Messages from angels are cheers about how wonderful and important each of us is. Angels want to release us from being self-absorbed; they want us to realize we are one big human family. If you don't care about yourself, you won't care about other humans on this planet. This isn't news; it is basic knowledge. When you feel good about who you are and where you are going, you automatically make the world a better place to be by your right and decent actions. You automatically recognize your universal responsibility to have deep respect and concern for all, regardless of belief, race, nationality, or gender. This happens naturally when you set out on a positive self-transformative journey with the angels.

About the Structure of This Book

Each chapter in this book begins with a basic concept, then gives two or three "angel practices" to encourage personal growth along the lines of the main concept. A practice is a habitual action or repeated exercise to improve our skill at something. When athletes or musicians practice an activity over and over, their goal is to get to the point where they do not have to think about what they are doing. Their minds lead, and their bodies follow. Repeating a practice is a way of programming the mind. I'm sure you have come across the idea of programming the human mind at some time. It is a powerful technique. Positively programming your mind through spiritual practices will bring beneficial results such as happiness, success, and the art of being your true self.

Part One of this book focuses on strengthening and listening to your inner wisdom and discovering your higher gifts. You will learn how to communicate with the angels through your thoughts and with your trust.

In Part Two of this book, you will find out how angels can help you tap into the empowerment brought by positive thinking. You will learn to change brain programs and habits and reprogram yourself into the positive. Change is not easy, because it clashes with old, habitual ways of doing things and outdated beliefs that play over and over again in our minds. To progress on our path, we must allow changes in our basic character. To effectively practice positive thinking means eliminating negative beliefs.

Part Three of this book touches on the themes of recovery and wisdom. It begins with a chapter about angels and the Twelve-Step programs that originated with Alcoholics Anonymous (A.A.) and that have inspired many other self-help groups based on these principles. I find the twelve steps valuable simply because they describe ways to work with universal elements of the spiritual journey. There is a genius behind these steps. If you follow them, you are on a spiritual path. Even if you've never heard of the twelve steps but are on a spiritual path, you have encountered the issues the steps embody. I included this chapter so people can begin to allow the angels to help them with the twelve steps if they are in one of the programs. The other two chapters in Part Three focus on our relationship with ourselves and our inner wise angel, and our relationships with other humans.

Part Four of this book includes chapters on faith, hope, grace, optimism, and forgiveness/understanding. These accelerators of growth move us along when we open our lives to them. Self-forgiveness as an accelerator opens our hearts to the angels; it proclaims that we are ready to love ourselves and treat ourselves as the truly beautiful humans we are. This in turn makes us available to receive all of the wondrous gifts the angels have to give us.

Part Five of this book is about bringing nonattachment into our lives as a constant practice, and also about freeing our inner angel child. You will learn to free yourself of your excess baggage; it will leave you when you release your hold on it.

The last part of the book, Part Six, looks at how we can begin to go outside the limited confines of our bodies and emotions and find our true place among others in the world. Giving our own brand of love to the world through service is the highest form of spiritual living we can practice. As we serve God, the angels guide us so that our giving is effortless. When we truly know and trust ourselves, we become spiritual teachers for others. We may not know exactly how we are teaching others or how many we really reach, but this doesn't matter; by becoming vehicles of light, we send positive reverberations throughout the universe, transmuting the negative. We learn to "find God in ourselves instead of going after the devil in others."

Part One
Inner Angel Guidance

About Part One:

How to Talk to Angels

Realize the great truth that each of us is a droplet of divinity,
a spiritual being housed in a temple, the body, which enables
us to operate in the heavy density of the material world. We
have become so imbued with the "onlooker consciousness"
that we too easily assume that God or our guides will speak
to us from outside. But the great truth is that the beings of the
higher worlds speak to us within our own thinking. All is
thought; in thinking we blend with higher beings.

Sir George Trevelyan

Many people want to know how to talk to angels and how to
get angels to talk to them. Angels speak to us through our
thoughts. To listen and talk to angels, we must become familiar
with our thoughts and our minds. We must go within and connect with the silent peace that resides at the center of our being. This may not be what people want to hear. It would be easier
if angels always materialized and spoke to us the way other humans do, giving us clear directions to follow to make our dreams
come true. But direct physical encounters of this kind might

interfere with our exercise of free will; we might lose sight of our own role as cocreators. So to connect with the angels, our cocreative counterparts, we first have to create the proper climate of trust for the connection. The climate of trust must emanate from within. We can't go outside of ourselves to find it. Clear communication with the angels is possible as we train our minds and learn about who we are inside, as we learn to identify with our higher self.

Training your mind in this way is a very simple process. You don't need to do anything fancy or be at a "high" spiritual level. All you need to do is trust yourself and practice the attitudes of the angels, such as taking yourself lightly, going lightly through life, thinking positively, nurturing hope, practicing and meditating on self-love, being kind in your thoughts and actions, and realizing that the angels love you unconditionally. The angels help anyone who asks and anyone who aspires to their ideals. The only thing angels don't help humans do is destroy themselves, the planet, and other humans; they are always a force for all that is positive, good, and true.

The chapters in Part One deal with creating a climate of peace and inner strength. You will learn to develop your internal self to be as strong as, or stronger than, your external self. You will learn to tap into a deep connection within yourself at any time, to find that place inside where you are guided by the angels you have called to you, and to use this connection appropriately. The practices in Part One are designed to help you get in touch with the light that glows within your soul, to help you to brighten that light so you are a beacon of hope shining for the world around you.

Angel practices are exercises to strengthen your inner being, just as physical exercises strengthen your body. Following these practices will give you the spiritual perseverance so necessary in the modern world. You will learn to bring your heavenly companions, the angels, with you on your spiritual path, the road less traveled, taking it one step at a time.

It's All in Your Mind

Think for a moment about where your mind is located, what your mind is, and what is in it. Some languages have no exact word for mind. Our own definitions are probably as varied as our personal beliefs. I don't intend to define the mind in this book, but I will be touching on many experiences that take place in the mind, such as thoughts, through which the angels speak to us. To give us a common framework, I offer here some general comments on the nature of the mind based on my studies and intuition.

Our minds are responsible for feelings, intelligence, reason, perceptions, judgments, and awareness of self—all of which depend on memory. Most functions of the mind relate back to memory in some way.

The operation of the mind in our physical body depends on the brain, just as the operation of our physical body depends on the brain. I believe that our minds are our direct connection to heaven. I like to think of our minds as being hooked up to our bodies on one end and hooked up to heaven, or divine cosmic consciousness, on the other.

Our brains are receivers or homes for our minds. Our minds prefer to seek out higher realms, to make contact with the angels. This is why we humans perpetually quest for the spiritual and do not feel complete until we know the higher power in our lives. This also means that our expanded minds are available for direct communication with the angels. Of course, as I've mentioned earlier, angels will not interfere with our lives and our thoughts; they only inspire us and instill noble thoughts into our minds if we give them permission. One important gift the angels have for our minds is hope. Hope keeps us directed toward the future with a positive outlook.

Chapter 1

Uniting Angelic and Human Energy

We devas would like to dance around in the consciousness of every human being to wake you up to what you are. We would have you know that you are light beings and not confined to your physical presence. Simply because you think that you are so confined, you remain so, but when you are aware of us and come to our level, you are part of a larger world which is also home to you. So join us often to be educated about yourself, and do it in the love of the One.

Message from the Tree Devas received by Dorothy Maclean

A story is told about the Buddha meeting up with a yogi who bragged he could walk across a river on top of the water, which meant his spiritual powers were greater than the Buddha's. The yogi proved that he could walk on water and said it took him at least twenty-five years of strict spiritual training to master this power. The Buddha scratched his head and asked why he had bothered, since for a mere five rupees the yogi could have taken the ferry.

5

When people find out I wrote a book about angels, they often ask, "Are *you* an angel?" and "Have you ever seen an angel?" I get the feeling that they would like me to enter a state of rapture and proclaim that an angel appeared to me in the brightest light possible, so intense I could hardly stand up, and the angel told me to write a book so people could have this same experience. Then I get the feeling they are a little disappointed because I have no sensational claims to make, no explanation for how I hide my wings. To answer these questions truthfully: First, I am a human and proud of it. Second, I have not seen an angel in the full regalia of heaven. I have seen things happen that could only have been done by an angel, and I have met a few people that I am almost certain were angels posing as humans, but this sense didn't dawn on me until after the meeting was over and I usually couldn't find the people again to ask if they really were angels. I would rather have angels leave subtle clues of their existence, which when I discover them strengthen my inner growth; this is more important than external events or a physical visit.

The story about the Buddha and the yogi that opens this chapter demonstrates how we can get carried away with so-called miracles and ignore what we need to do in everyday life. After all, we are only human—and that in and of itself is a miracle! Angels don't have to come in a rapture to give us a message, and they usually won't. Even if they do, this doesn't mean our spiritual powers are any greater than before. If we look for signs and wonders as the only way to know angels (and to grow spiritually), we may miss the message altogether. Of course, angels do help cocreate miracles in the lives of humans. We all have different experiences of life, and the ways angels work in our lives will be personal to us.

As a culture, we seem to need intensity to feel we are alive. Boredom is our biggest fear. We want to be entertained and in awe; when we don't get this, we are apt to go out of our way to find it. This need for entertainment affects all areas of our lives, from relationships to food and clothing, and it is often extended to our spiritual path as well. When something is new, it is exciting and intense, but after a while the excitement wears off because we get used to it. The unfortunate side effect of this addiction to entertainment is that when people want to *feel* so much, they sometimes settle for feeling pain and suffering and self-hatred.

The way out of this trap is to learn to endure the voids and the days of impasse, the days you feel "nothing," the days boredom looms at every turn and you think the angels have taken a vacation. There is really nothing bad about a day of nonfeeling. You can easily turn it around to become a time of cultivation and inner preparation for other, richer experiences. On the "nothing" days, remember that the angels are not on vacation; in fact, they may be very busy playing with your mind and helping you reprogram your thoughts for the fun times ahead. So relax and accept a day or two, now and then, when things aren't exactly fun and exciting.

We all experience angels in our own ways; it's best not to compare and judge such experiences based on how sensational and intense they are. Each experience is as important as any other. One reason I don't use a lot of angel stories to prove the existence of angels is that I don't want people to get a preconceived notion of what an angel experience has to be like or, worse, to be sad because they have never had such an experience. I don't share some of my angel experiences because I feel they are meant for my stage of learning and would lose too much in the translation into words. My friend Shannon once said, "The reason it is difficult to tell someone about an angel experience is that you really do 'have to be there.' So much happens within a sort of time warp, colors may look different, one's senses are heightened, and the situation usually hits a deep note of humor that may only be meant for you personally." I would love to relay some of the hilarity the angels have provided in my life, but words just won't do it. So be there in the moment when you have an angel experience; I cannot tell you how or where it will happen, but go with the divine humor in the situation and you will be overcome by mirth.

My approach to angel consciousness is to allow for expansion, mine and yours, and to be practical. By being practical, I mean that I want to offer you real practices that can be used to open your heart to the angels in your own way and at your own pace. I am not out to change your beliefs. I am glad we all have our own belief systems. Think of how boring it would be if we all believed the same things and everyone we met agreed with us! This said, I invite you to further expand and explore your personal awareness of angels.

Practice 1: Angel Alpha State

To do inner spiritual work, we must learn to create a climate in our minds that will allow us to be still and listen to our inner guidance. Our inner guidance involves listening to our higher self, our guardian angel, and our spiritual guides with the innocence of a little child. It also involves raising our level to be one with our higher self and guardians and guides. This exercise helps you practice attuning with the light energy, joining with the angels, and learning about yourself. Our society has not placed a high value on spiritual insight and spiritual listening. This lack of focus on the spiritual dimension is changing every day, in all fields of endeavor, but we still have a long way to go. We need a balance of action and contemplation. We are a society that has been looking for fulfillment from the outside in, rather than the inside out. Many people claim they feel empty, as if there was something missing. This feeling can be healed by going inside and becoming aware of what is missing and realizing what you want to fill the space with.

Because the angel alpha state you will learn here is useful for all of the practices in this book, I have made it the first practice. Angel alpha state uses the alpha waves our brains naturally produce in a certain state of consciousness. There are four classes of brain waves—alpha, beta, theta, and delta. These four classes indicate the different frequencies, or numbers of cycles per second, of the brain waves. Delta waves are the slowest of all, zero to four cycles per second; they are most prominent when you are so deeply asleep you are not even dreaming. Theta brain waves, four to eight cycles per second, are related to drowsiness, creativity, and dream time. Beta waves are the fastest, running thirteen to twenty-six cycles per second; they signal the state of normal wakefulness. Alpha waves are half that of the beta waves, about eight to thirteen cycles per second. Alpha waves are connected with a relaxed, yet alert, mental state. We go through the alpha state right before we fall asleep and right before we awaken. Alpha brain waves predominate when we meditate. They are the key to a peaceful mind and a feeling of centeredness; they are our true friends.

Whenever you want to reach angel alpha state, take a few deep breaths, relax your body, and simply connect with the center of your mental peace. Feel the alpha waves roll gently through your brain. If you like, use the word *angel* as a mantra. Tell your mind you want to connect with the vibration level and light level of the angelic kingdom. Program your mind ahead of time to cultivate innocence or other virtuous qualities. When you use angel alpha for other practices in the book, read through the practice and then program that practice into your mind. To program, simply tell your mind what virtue or practice you want to cultivate in your meditation, then get out of the way—that is, don't think or try to concentrate to keep it going. Such efforts constitute thinking, and you want to go beyond the thinking stage and listen to the angels. Your meditation may take you in a different direction than you expected, but that is fine. With practice, you will sharpen your ability to program.

As you practice angel alpha, you will discover the method that works best for you. You don't have to be at any particular spiritual level or be a regular practitioner of meditation to use angel alpha state; the angels see to it that you can slow your brain waves down and join them for a moment of mental peace. There are no set rules; basically, you just need to relax and not push for anything sensational to happen. Learn to take short time-outs and call forth angel alpha waves when you need them, whenever things seem to be getting out of hand.

Remember that angels are messengers from God. When you meditate in alpha state, declare and realize that you are listening to the kingdom of God, the higher power in your life. Your higher power is personal to you, but a good testing point when listening to God and the angels is that the messages never cause fear. Messages from the angels always use the right timing and encourage happiness.

Practice 2: Playing With Angel Light

Light can increase your vibration, amplify the strength of your positive thoughts, and open your heart. You can link with it, harness its power, and create good all around you.

Orin, as channeled by Sanaya Roman

The angels are beings of light, possessing all the psychological qualities of light itself. In her book *Spiritual Growth*, Sanaya Roman talks about light as a potent force of transformation. She also says that we can bring more light into our lives by thinking of it. "Light responds to your thought of it; as you think of it, it is immediately drawn to you." This is the same with angels; they respond to our thoughts of them, and we can call them to us by thinking of them. When you send someone light, you are sending angels, and when you surround yourself in white light, you are surrounding yourself with angel energy. Visualizing yourself encompassed in light (white for transformation and rose pink for love vibrations) illuminates and raises the vibration around you.

When I speak of light in this book, I'm referring to the light of the highest love force in the universe — the light of the divine, of God. This light is the true spark of life. It is what glows in our souls. It is the substance of our higher self, our life force. It is the light in en*light*enment, the light that dawns on us. It is the truth that allows us to "see the light." Phrases such as "in light of this" and "to throw light on this" are used to help make something clearer or more lucid. When we see something in a "different light," our perception of the situation has changed. We hear the term "living in the light" a lot these days to indicate living in a state of spiritual awareness, as opposed to living in the darkness that represents the negative, problematic denial of the spiritual side of our nature. Paintings depict angels with a halo of light surrounding them. Saints and holy people of numerous religions are also surrounded by halos. It is fun to begin playing with light ideas, exploring the whole idea of light and how the word is used and its many meanings. Another favorite connotation of the word *light* is nonserious, weightless, not tied down to the earth with heavy thoughts and feelings.

Why is it that more people are afraid of the dark than they are of the light? Some of the words opposite to light and representing darkness are blackness, murkiness, soullessness, depression, sadness, shady, sinister, dismal, and somber. These words often indicate some sort of lie or misconception. Darkness is fairly easy to get rid of; we simply have to turn on the light. The trick is that we must keep the light on; we must bring a kind of daylight into our mind and stay awake. We need a daily practice to keep the climate in our mind bright and sunny by focusing our thoughts on light and love.

When you are feeling low, take a quick "light bath." Sit quietly for a moment, close your eyes, and focus on the light inside your mind. Concentrate on light with your eyes closed for a moment and don't open your eyes until it is daylight in your mind — whatever that means to you, as long as it is a positive, enlightening experience. Ask the angels to join the light you are generating. Ask the angels to protect your light and allow you to use it in various ways. One way to use your light is for healing. If you have pain somewhere in your body, use a beam of your angel light and focus it on the cells surrounding the area of pain or sickness. Imagine the light becoming a potent healing force originating from the light of the healing angels. Feel the sparkling golden light entering your cells and permeating the tissue; feel the effervescence of empowerment. Use this practice to send the beam to others you know who might be suffering. Visualize a laser beam of white healing light sparkling with gold flecks of God dust that you can direct wherever you choose.

Remember to use light to strengthen your positive thoughts. If you are feeling depressed or unloved, use this angel light to let you know you are truly loved in heaven, and ask the angel happiness trainers to smile on you. We often forget that the best loving help for us is not available on earth (in the form of other humans, toys, entertainment) but is abundant in heaven. This is easy to forget since as humans we get so entangled with other people and with human institutions, such as our workplaces. The more you use heaven's help, the happier you will be and the more fulfilled you will feel.

Angels are always available to cheer you on to be your best possible self. They are also very forgiving if you forget about them. The key here is to ask for their love light to shine *on* you, *through* you, and *around* you. Then get creative: The light is yours to play with and can only be used for your highest good and the highest good of all around you. So you won't go wrong when you play with angel light. Let's face the light and use it in our lives. Light is very positive energy and is free for the asking.

Practice 3: Combining Energy Systems With Your Guardian Angel's

We have a guardian angel who is always with us. Many people become aware of their guardian angel when they are in danger, and a force outside themselves rescues them or guides them to safety. It's all right if you haven't yet recognized the times in your life when your guardian was with you; you can begin your awareness starting now. As you open your mind, you may find yourself remembering long-forgotten incidents from your past that relate to your own guardian angel. Such memories don't always concern moments of danger. In fact, most of the experiences we have with our angels are wonderful peak experiences of joy, love, and happiness. Perhaps you remember a time when you felt good for no reason and wanted to laugh and sing, or a time when you had a life-transforming inspiration, followed it, and everything went well. Maybe as a child you were alone and afraid and a beautiful light appeared and made you feel safe and at home on the planet. When identifying angel experiences, don't be too strict with yourself or concentrate too heavily on divine miracles in which angels appear and fly you off to safety. Just be yourself, and you will know how and when your guardian angel has helped you. You will begin to see all the creative and fun experiences you and your guardian can generate now that you know each other. Basically, I'm suggesting that you become best friends with your guardian angel! Pretend you have an invisible best friend who witnesses everything you experience and with whom you can share insights.

People have different ideas about guardian angels. Some people think their guardian angel is their higher self, part of the same energy system as their own soul or spirit. Others think their guardian angel is a separate being who stands behind them at all times. Other people call their guardian angel their spirit guide. Choose the explanation that fits best for you; even if you have doubts, try to keep an open mind and little by little you will get to know your guardian angel.

When a situation in my life warrants special empowerment, I imagine my energy system in complete alignment with my guardian angel's. I do this when I want to expand my consciousness or receive valuable insights. Aligning your energy system with your guardian angel's is also good for giving you a dose of healing energy. There are no rules to this; simply use your own feelings about your guardian angel and allow it to happen. Finding a quiet place and going into angel alpha state may help. This practice doesn't have to require time-consuming effort; you may just need a brief moment of alignment. The key here is not to judge what is happening. The insight or healing you are asking for may come later when you least expect it. Sometimes I feel a sensation of light enter my body and expand until my entire body feels as though it is changing into light. Then the sensation leaves and I feel refreshed and renewed, and I have more clarity for what I'm doing. Again, the angelic realm never causes fear, never gives you negative instructions, and always leaves you feeling lighter and better about yourself — and much happier.

Chapter 2

Cleaning the Window of Your Soul

If one ever has the good fortune to meet a living saint, one will have then met someone absolutely unique. Though their visions may be remarkably similar, the personhood of saints is remarkably different. This is because they have become utterly themselves. God creates each soul differently, so that when all the mud is finally cleared away, His light will shine through it in a beautiful, colorful, totally new pattern.

M. Scott Peck, People of the Lie

A saint (an authentic human being) is someone who is free of the weight and mud of darkness and negativity. At the core of our souls resides our gift (our sainthood), alive and real, unique and special, powerful and transforming. When we clean away the mud from our souls, our gifts are visible and we give of ourselves in all our actions. Soul or saint making is not an overnight process; it may take most of our lives, or it may take only a few revelations of the truth—it all depends on who we are and what we

15

are dealing with. That is why it is so important to have respect for one another. Finding the gifts at the core of our soul is an interesting process. It frees us to be truly ourselves in the most beautiful light available, God's love.

This book is about cleaning the mud from our souls, with the help of our angels, so that we are able to enjoy the freedom of happiness and creativity. This chapter concerns the purification of our souls. The word *purification* has always made me a little uneasy; the concept can seem so overwhelming and perfectionistic. I immediately think of diets, fasting, restrictions—in other words, of a lot of work. In contrast, when the angels teach about purification, they just mean "becoming purely you," free of negative habits and negative perceptions.

Again and again, I have mentioned the idea of a spiritual path. When we choose to travel a spiritual path, we have decided to find out about ourselves, to discover our unique way of contributing love to the world, and to understand at a deeper level that we are all connected. We are pieces of a beautiful mosaic, the big picture, the web of life. I use the term *spiritual* to indicate choosing to develop a knowledge of our soul and spirit, our link with the higher power and the kingdom of God—choosing to develop a clear view of the color of our own special heart light, to know exactly who we are. A nonspiritual path entails taking care of physical needs, material success, and worldly recognition (all of which can be a part of a spiritual path, too) but not doing any work on inner growth.

Once we are traveling on a spiritual path, we begin to recognize that we are spiritual beings having a human experience. Negative patterns such as guilt, shame, self-hatred, laziness, pride, greed, fear, and anger can interfere with our spiritual growth. These patterns compose the mud that cakes onto the window of our soul, blocking our own special light. These patterns chip away at our integrity. Our integrity requires us to go through lessons that may be painful, but each time the roller coaster of life takes a dip and we stick with it, we end up back on top with more power and hope to endure the low times. To prepare us for these inevitable ups and downs, a spiritual life involves many practices and conscious clear thinking. We may be taking different courses, each in our unique way, but the true and noble search for truth on the spiritual path leads all of us to the same ultimate destination.

Practice 1: Visualizing the Angel Soul Window Cleaners

You are the light of the world.

Matthew 5:14

Picture God as an enormous diamond, cut perfectly with infinite facets. From each facet shines a unique pattern of light, more beautiful and magnificent than any color visible on earth. The light of each facet is focused on one human being. This light is the light of the gift we have to offer to the world; it is the light that unites us to God and to each other. We are all part of a spectrum consisting of beautiful colors. When we are free to be ourselves, our light shines from our souls in a bright, unique pattern. Our light shines most brightly at the times we are truly ourselves.

One way to recognize the mud or dust that hides your light is to take an honest look at yourself and identify the patterns that cause you self-doubt and unhappiness. To do this, take a quiet moment to meditate. Enter angel alpha state, and, when you feel ready, start to go within and connect with your light color. You may not see an absolute color as such, so concentrate on your own center of energy — the source of you. Ask the angels to show you some of the mud or dust that is dulling your brilliance. Pay attention, and when something pops into your mind that you want to eliminate, visualize angel window cleaners spraying the spot or clump with a cleaning solution and watch it vanish out into the universe to be transmuted. Be creative, and if you are keeping a journal write about the experience so you can review it every once in a while.

The angels help us stay authentic and true to ourselves. They do this in many ways, because the angels around us hold the blueprint, or design, we helped create before we came into existence. When we get too far away from our center, the angels leave subtle clues to remind us to get back on course and be ourselves. It isn't easy to be ourselves all the time. When we face routine situations, we may start behaving as if we were on automatic pilot. We discover who we are and what automatic programs are operating in our lives through self-awareness. When we become aware of a pattern, we give ourselves a choice either to continue it or not. And even when we choose to continue the pattern, it changes because we are more aware of what we are doing.

The theme of this practice is to become authentic; the joke is that there is no special trick or key to becoming authentic! Authenticity values how unique each of us is. So you may have to alter some of the practices in this book so they fit your own soul better. Authenticity comes from truly knowing yourself. "Know yourself and you will know how to live" the saying goes. Once you know yourself, you will know how to give of yourself. If we cannot give of ourselves, the condition of self-obsession takes hold and knowing ourselves may backfire. If this happens, just hang in there and ask the angels to remind you who you are and what you are here to do. Then *do it* and you will have more fun than you could ever have imagined.

Practice 2: The Power of Transmission

When we are truly ourselves, we broadcast a message of love that creates a positive chain reaction in the universe. Just walking by someone on the street could change that person's life. We can give other humans the experience of angels without knowing it in the same way that we receive angelic experiences around certain people and wonder if they are angels. Sometimes when we try to give messages to others, they miss them; then, when we aren't trying at all, the message is broadcast loud and clear. One way to encourage positive transmissions is to send them out, by radiating your light and the light of the angels. You can do this by consciously sending blessings on beams of light or angel wings to a certain person, place, or group.

You can also broadcast a message that you want to attract the people who need you most and who you need the most in your life. This is naturally taken care of when you are expressing to the world around you who you really are. Be aware and conscious of what you are transmitting and remember: When in doubt, be charming, and broadcast a program of delight and joy.

Practice 3: Defining the Moment

Sometimes when I am clouded over by worries and negative thoughts, I find a quiet spot where I will be alone, get my journal out, and start writing. I write down anything that is happening in the present, including my worries, fears, happy thoughts, and the temperature of the room and how it affects me. If I am inside the house, I write about what is happening outside the window. I write about the sounds I hear and what the room smells like. I note how the light is playing in the room. I write about how tired, nervous, tense, relaxed, or numb my body feels. In other words, I try to define my entire experience in the present, including all the things that take me out of the present, such as worries. By writing down everything you are experiencing, you will discover many interesting things. First, you may discover you change from happy thoughts to sad or uncomfortable thoughts very quickly. You are not necessarily frozen in any one mood, as we are sometimes led to believe. Second, you may uncover the very essence of what is worrying you; then you can begin to brainstorm about possible solutions. Finally, if you allow your mind to wander completely freely, strange thoughts may surface and memories may pop up for no apparent reason. Don't judge or analyze; just record your experience of the present—noting all the sensations you are experiencing.

After you have done this for a while, ask the angels to take free reign in your mind. To make sure it is the angels you are allowing in, surround yourself with the white, golden pink light of the angelic realm. Declare that only the presence of the kingdom of God, only the Christ consciousness, is welcome. All you have to do is ask that angels surround you; the rest is just reassurance to pacify your doubts and fears. Now, repeat all the steps you did before, recording the present without judging, comparing, controlling, or trying. Especially pay attention to and record any new awarenesses you have concerning a particular situation, or any new ideas that come to you. These could lead to solutions and creative encounters at a later time.

This exercise also helps free the writer within you, the everyday journalist who dwells in your mind. Practicing this technique leads to great self-awareness; the more you do it, the more interesting it gets. But, please, don't try to channel angels; this is not what I am talking about. The channeling process that has become so popular is totally different from recording thoughts and sensations the angels give you. If you start to receive verbose details and detailed belief systems, I suggest you stop. When you are dealing with angels, they do not interfere with your free will, and they don't offer you a set belief system. Angels simply inspire you, and they don't always use words or phrases to do this. You can transcribe these messages into words in your mind or imagination, and they will be sweet and comforting to your soul.

Another reason this exercise is so useful is that it can help you uncover unfinished business. Unfinished business consists of unexpressed emotions, events, and memories that linger on in our minds. Through constant everyday avoidance, we often try to escape from the feelings that must be felt in order to release the unfinished business of unexpressed feelings or blocked emotions.

The most direct way to deal with unfinished business is to confront the person or situation related to it. If this isn't possible, there are other effective ways to deal with unfinished business. You can write letters to people you have unfinished business with (whether they are still alive on the physical planet or have passed on) and to their highest angels (sometimes you may choose to send the completed letter; other times it may be more appropriate to burn it or file it in your journal). Another way of dealing with unfinished business is to explore the situation with someone you trust, such as a therapist or a good friend. Sometimes, just the act of acknowledging the unfinished business and declaring the desire to finish it will be enough to free you.

Exploring the present through this practice is a good way to start cleaning the window of your soul. You will see on paper things that may be blocking the special God light that glows within your heart and soul, waiting for the chance to shine out clear and bright.

Chapter 3

Angel Pain Transformers

*You will not grow if you sit in a beautiful flower garden
and somebody brings you gorgeous food on a silver platter.
But you will grow if you are sick, if you are in pain, if you
experience losses, and if you do not put your head in the
sand, but take the pain and learn to accept it, not as a
curse or a punishment, but as a gift to you with a very,
very specific purpose.*

Elisabeth Kübler-Ross

At the beginning of this book, I suggested that one of the main
reasons you are reading this book may be to increase your happiness. This is indeed a noble reason and one I truly respect,
because happiness extends itself — it expands outward and benefits many. Another reason you may be interested in this book
is that you are sick of pain and suffering and want a shortcut
to avoid it; maybe in the back of your mind you believe angels
can provide such a shortcut.

When I was eleven years old and a proud member of the Girl
Scouts, I learned a valuable lesson about shortcuts. Our troop

was hiking down a steep mountain trail with many switchbacks. I always liked the idea of being first down the mountain, so I usually hurried a little, and this time was no exception. I had a friend with me and we were making good time until I found what I thought to be a shortcut bypassing one of the switchbacks on the trail. It was a steep part of the mountain that led straight down to the continuing trail, and I convinced my friend that we could make it if we sat down and inched our way carefully.

Everything was going fine until a group of Boy Scouts arrived on the scene and decided we were stuck on the mountain. They had been studying rescue techniques and, having immediately recognized the emergency of two girls stuck on a mountain, quickly went into action to save us. Of course, they ignored my ranting and raving that we were fine and could make it down the mountain ourselves, and in no time at all were climbing the mountain to save us. The most humiliating moment was when the rest of our troop showed up, leaders and all, to join the other spectators. When they finally got us off the mountain, I felt deflated and embarrassed and the brave Boy Scouts who "saved" us looked like heroes.

What I learned from this experience is that there is no short-cut in life; a path is a path. I learned that if we take a shortcut to avoid pain, suffering, or effort, we usually end up making more work for ourselves and worse pain than if we just stayed on the path and went through the suffering we were trying to avoid. Look at all the people who got involved in my shortcut and the roles they played—heroes, victims, spectators, and sympathizers. Sometimes, when we postpone suffering and repress feelings that cause us pain, thinking we are taking a shortcut, others are also affected by our decision.

Unfortunately, there are no true shortcuts on the spiritual path. Angels do not provide shortcuts, but they can help us face the truth of situations and can help us learn the value of facing problems directly. Angels help us see the necessity of suffering at certain times. The wonderful thing about angels is that they are always there with us; we are definitely not alone. When we examine our troubles, the angels help us look for the positive in all situations, helping us keep our sense of humor at all times. And they remind us when it is time to let go of the suffering and start enjoying life.

Angels are available to help us look at the workings of our own minds and to recognize the patterns and shortcuts we incorporate that keep us from living happily. Angels can be good psychotherapists, guiding us to look inside ourselves for answers and insights. I'm certainly not suggesting that you avoid human psychotherapists; if you are working with a therapist, or thinking about it, I suggest you take along your angel psychotherapist. You'll be surprised at the amazing growth that takes place when you combine human and angelic forces.

Practice 1: Angels and Pain Relief

Oh my Lord! How true it is that whoever works for You is paid in troubles! And what a precious price to those who love You if we understand its value.

                                                    St. Teresa of Avila

Human beings do some clever and not-so-clever things to avoid suffering and pain. It is not hard to understand why we want to avoid feelings of pain and frustration. Grief, anger, loneliness, regret, rejection, fear, despair, and hate are not fun experiences. To avoid these experiences, some of us procrastinate and ignore, hoping things will work themselves out without any effort on our part; take drugs to deaden the pain; surround ourselves with too much work so we never have the time to deal with pain; become severely depressed; and live in fantasy worlds or in the past or in the future. All of these defenses against pain keep us from experiencing life in the moment. I'm sure you've heard about the importance of living in the moment, but this simple truth bears repetition because the moment is really the only time we have. You may have heard it said that our worst troubles are those that never happen; in other words, they only exist in our imagination. We take up valuable space in our imagination worrying about something that will never happen. The unpleasant experiences of life don't have to be so bad if they are dealt with in the present tense. Living fully in the present can be fascinating; it all depends on what attitude you have toward it.

Our society is bent on getting rid of pain; we seek quick relief, the quicker the better. If we have a slight headache, a commercial on T.V. reminds us to take a pill right away to get rid of it. We are so convinced that pain is bad that when we have pain in our lives we feel like failures.

I can't claim to know what it is like to feel every type of suffering this world has to offer. When I hear about the shocking experiences some people have had to live through, I cannot possibly comprehend what it was like. But one thing I do know is that if we use our own pain as a lesson or positive turning point in our lives, it can be the most valuable lesson we could ever imagine, leading us to greatness. Dr. Bernie Siegel refers to pain and suffering as "God's reset button," a message for us to rethink our path, maybe change our character and destiny, and "find our own special way to contribute love to the world."

If there is pain in your life and body, ask the angels to help you understand the higher meaning it has for your life path. Ask the angels to lead you to the true source of your pain and give you insights on how to relieve it naturally and for your own highest good. If a situation in your life is too painful to look at honestly, meaning if there is something in your life you are not willing to face yet because you feel alone, know you are not alone. The angels are right there with you; when you are ready to admit something painful to yourself, they will admire and reward you for doing so.

Take a different view of pain. What exactly is pain, and why is it so awful? Why is it so difficult to watch another human suffer? What would you do if someone you loved was suffering pain from a terminal disease and asked you to help him or her die? Why does suicide create so much anger for those left behind? Do these questions mean anything to you? Or would you rather avoid them? I ask these questions because sometimes we take on other people's pain and end up judging the situation from our point of view. We may think to ourselves, Why doesn't that person just get better and live? When you experience pain, take an angel instead of a pain killer. Use your journal and ask yourself, Am I avoiding a supposed painful situation? Have I been tolerating a low-grade form of pain in order to avoid a shorter spurt of intense pain? Formulate a request, then send it out to the angels, stating that you are willing to clearly view the reason pain is in your life. Then receive your help from above.

Practice 2: Remaining Centered With Humor Time-outs

This exercise helps you develop a system of healing your mental state with humor and developing a maintenance plan for a centered mind. Gravity prevails here on earth, and there are many opportunities for us to weigh ourselves down. The basic philosophy of this practice is to lighten up and get rid of mental gravity. To be truly healthy mentally, we must take a hundred honest looks at ourselves each day. With the angels on our side, we can see the humor in our situation, and with each honest look at ourselves we can have a good laugh; seriousness and gravity naturally vanish.

Whenever you are able during the day, take a time-out to laugh at yourself, or with yourself. Look at the potential for humor in whatever situation you are dealing with. The best comedy is real life, especially when people are going about their business and beginning to take themselves too seriously. Pride makes for a lot of humorous situations, so when you see signs of pride, in yourself or others, look for the humor it creates. Taking a time-out to lighten up and laugh helps you remain centered and true to yourself. Humor can change your perception in an instant. The ability to see humor in everyday experience helps immensely in coping with stress.

Humor strikes a different note in all of us. You find this out when you are trying to tell someone something funny that happened to you and you begin laughing so hard you can't finish the story, and the other person gives you a strange look. Then, when you finally finish the story, the person laughs mostly because you are laughing so hard. If you can't find a friend to laugh with, laugh with your angels. Who cares if someone sees you laughing by yourself? That in itself is funny. Have a laugh fest. For a few Sunday nights in a row, I watched some really silly comedy shows on T.V.; inevitably something struck me as humorous and I would start laughing so hard I couldn't stop myself. The interesting thing is that the parts of the shows that made me laugh were so absurd, they probably were not what the writers considered funny. I can only say that having a laugh fest on Sunday night is great, because you get rid of all sorts of seriousness the night before your week begins, so you are ready to face it in a much lighter state.

The easiest way to bring more humor into your life is to ask the angels to provide it. Declare to the angels that you are sick and tired of seriousness and that you are ready and willing to accept more humor in your life. Wake up in the morning and proclaim the fact that you will laugh today and have many light moments and that your guardian angels will help you with this. Develop your own maintenance plan to keep your mind open to the absurd and ridiculous experiences of life. If you are choking on pride, just relax and have a good laugh, make an ass out of yourself, and go with it. When the unexpected happens and throws you off a bit, learn to pause for a beat and look for the humor. Take an honest look at yourself whenever possible and do it with love and humor and you will live for a very long time! Remember to enjoy yourself at least a little each day; the angels will help and support you one hundred percent.

Practice 3: Healing the Body/Mind

Although most of the chapters in this book concentrate on the mind, the body is always involved. The mind is much more powerful than the body, but they work together. A healthy body usually means a healthy mind and vice versa. The body/mind connection runs deep and can manifest in ways you may not want to believe because it defies reason.

Looking objectively at disease or sickness can sometimes put the whole thing into perspective. In high school, I was involved in a Gestalt therapy group. Whenever one of us was sick with a cold, our leader would ask us why we needed the cold. At first I thought she was being strange, because colds come from a virus and we have no control over getting them. When I looked more deeply at my own reasons for developing a cold now and then, her question began to make more sense. Sickness can be a positive experience leading to transformation. If you take care of yourself by looking honestly at why you got sick or diseased, and if you take positive steps toward healing, miracles can take place. When you bring in the angels, healing will involve all sorts of fun things always meant to bring you closer to home base — your true, special, authentic self.

The healing arts these days amaze me. There are so many choices. The angels are not prejudiced about any particular method, as long as it has the individual's highest good as its first priority. Angels know that the more strongly you believe in the method, the more effective it will be and the more the angels can help. I couldn't possibly name all of the healing systems and extraordinary books out today on healing. I personally like some of them more than others, but I also recognize that sometimes the method is not as important as the person's belief in the method and the healer. The most important aspect is that angels want you to be the best you possible, with a healthy mind full of mental peace and a healthy body full of sparkling energy. A graceful spirit does well in a graceful body. When true health touches you on all levels, your aliveness and vibrancy will be manifestations of the divine spirit in your body, your temple of God.

When you are choosing a healing art and healer, be intelligent. Treating serious diseases may take a combination of traditional and holistic medical systems. Be honest with yourself, and don't feel like a failure when you are sick or diseased. You are never a failure, and sickness means you are going through a transformation of some kind. Also, remember that death is not a failure. There is a divine master plan, and it is not up to us to decide when death is right or wrong. When people are dying, they need the utmost respect from themselves and others. Too often, when people get sick, other people project negative thoughts on them by taking the attitude that it is their fault that they are sick. Such an attitude shows a lack of compassion and unnecessary judgment; it is a projection of one's own fears. When people you know are sick, the best thing to do is to contact their angels and send them prayers of unconditional love. In the end, it is the love and compassion that truly heal, whether or not death is the outcome. And love can grow and expand far beyond death. People who have the courage to grow through pain and suffering in an awake and aware state are the bravest humans on this planet.

Because our bodies work in synch with our minds, most of the practices in this book can be used for physical healing as well as mental healing. The angels can play a big part in creating optimum health. It is up to you to bring them into your own picture of health in the way that is best for you. Know that angel light is very healing and of the highest vibration; use this light to cocreate sparkling health with the angels.

Chapter 4

Reckoning With Your Shadow

After all, angels are not perfectionists. One was, of course, but he fell from grace.

F. Forrester Church

All of us have a dark side — the shadow cast from the light. We all struggle with our dark side in our own unique ways. For a loose definition, we could say that the dark side of our personality is the side we often want to hide from the world. We keep it out of the light, and often try to deny it even exists, which makes the struggle much harder in the long run. Often we judge our dark side very harshly because it doesn't fit in with the persona we want the world to see. This can lead to pretending we are something we are not, or to denying the way our past history really took place.

Our dark side sometimes consists of character defects we hide away so we can feel safe. These defects are usually parts of ourselves we feel we have no real control over. At first, I did not like using the word *defect* because it sounds so permanent and final, but then I realized it really means imperfections. Thinking of defects as imperfections doesn't bother me as much because usually imperfections relate to our problems with control and our attempts to be perfect. I bought an Egyptian scarf recently with a fringe of beautiful purple beads; scattered throughout were a few green beads, which are referred to as the spirit beads (where the spirit enters the garment). The green beads represent the fact that none of us was made perfect. The Amish quilters also recognize this truth when they sew in a square of material that doesn't match the rest of the pattern just to remind us that God made no one perfect. The Navajos have a similar tradition.

Darkness is not synonymous with evil or bad. It sometimes represents these concepts, but our dark side or shadow is not necessarily "bad" or "evil." Evil can originate from and thrive on human fears such as the fear of pain and punishment, or fear of the dark. The fear of punishment keeps many of our imperfections locked up tight in the dark, where even we do not want to acknowledge them because then we believe we have to punish ourselves for them. A soul divided between dark and light remains weak; in contrast, the integrated soul is strong, centered, and fearless. To stop punishing ourselves, to integrate and overcome the parts of ourselves we are hiding, we need to look at the dark by turning on the light.

The light of truth allows us to look at our dark side and accept it as a part of our wholeness. Just as a small mirror can reflect light like a beacon, if our soul is bright with the light of truth, we will illuminate the dark with our own reflection and shine as a bright light of truth for the rest of the world. To remain centered and truly at peace within ourselves, we must practice self-honesty and discover our true essence and accept it. We must take off any masks we are wearing and ask the angels to guide us to an honest way of being. Angels are light; they will be with you when you look into the dark areas of your soul and they

will help you learn to love yourself and lighten up. True kindness and wisdom come from spiritual practice; there will always
be parts of yourself that work against the grain of kindness and
wisdom. The trick is to not get stuck along the way. Keep the
light of the angels on in your life, and they will teach you about
love that won't hurt and kindness that is free from expectations.

Practice 1: Playing With Projections

Have you ever had people get angry at you and start saying things
to you and about you that were so off base you wondered where
they were coming from and if they had mistaken you for someone else? If so, you have been the object of wild projections.
Projection is a defense mechanism we use to blame others for
our own faults or to assume that someone else feels the emotion that we are full of but don't want to face. In other words,
when we don't examine our shadow side, we may end up projecting it onto others. Becoming aware of projection tactics in ourselves and others will give us insight into the shadow side of
ourselves and others. If we can separate the hurt of an attack
and look at what people who are attacking us are projecting, we
can learn a lot about them and the space they are coming from.
We need to have high self-esteem and the integrity to see that
their projections are not really about us personally. Also, if we
listen to ourselves when we feel angry at others, we will learn
a lot about ourselves if we are brave enough to look honestly.

It is virtually impossible not to project. We see parts of ourselves in others and what we most notice in others, positive or
negative, are aspects of our own self. We all know that in order
to see our backside (representing our shadow), we need a mirror. There are parts of our personality that we can only see when
they are mirrored in some other person's personality, in other
words, when they are projected onto someone else.

Some people take the concept of projection very seriously.
In contrast, I advise that you lighten up and enjoy projection!

When you are the object of projection, realize that it is a gift of understanding, and don't get attached to what is being said about you. Practice detachment. When you yourself are projecting, learn to explore what you are projecting, and determine if it is hurtful to yourself and those around you. Awareness and awakeness leads to a natural progression of new choices and ways of being.

One way to explore and play with projections and your shadow side is to draw your monster. I use this technique with children to help them express their anger in a safe way. Children usually don't think twice about what I mean; they know they have a pet monster. Since we have a child within that sometimes feels anger, we, too, can benefit from drawing our monsters. Get a piece of paper and some crayons, colored markers, or pencils — using color is important for this exercise. Now draw your monster. Don't bother denying that you have one, because this exercise doesn't depend on whether you have a monster or not; you can draw your monster regardless of what you think. Don't worry about your art ability either; let yourself go — draw a stick monster or blobs of color if you want to. When you finish the drawing, make a caption and write about what your monster is angry about. Write this down as if you were the monster telling someone why you are angry. After you have finished writing, study your monster and some of the things it said. Where do the things your monster said originate? You may find all of them originate in a space of fear, or you may discover something different. Ask the angels for deeper insights and new ideas. Don't get too carried away with self-analysis; remember, we want to take this lightly because it is meant to be a safe expression of some anger or fear that we have been living with. Many of us have developed beliefs that if only we were perfect and didn't have awful thoughts, then our parents or spouses or whoever wouldn't behave a certain way. So we hide the thoughts in a closet. It's time to bring our monsters out of the closet and explore the awful thoughts, realize that they don't change others' behavior toward us, unless we lash out at them, and this we can learn to control.

Children have to be taught compassion and kindness in their actions, and ways to deal with their own anger constructively using self-control. In other words, we weren't born perfect; we were born with certain aspects of ourselves that are a struggle; by honest spiritual practice, we can overcome these aspects, and they will strengthen us. By using the right exercise or practice, our weakest point can become our greatest strength. We won't overcome our weaknesses if we hide them away and deny our feelings, regardless of what they are. When we start to feel brave enough to look at our dark side without judging ourselves as bad, we will learn ways to illuminate the darkness. Bring in the angels to stand next to you while you view your dark side; in the angels' light, the hidden aspects of our personalities don't look so serious and insurmountable. When we face the light and the angels, and go on our path with them, we won't be controlled by the shadows anymore. For when we turn toward the angels' light, it illuminates the shadows and we see what is there and know we have the capacity to transform the darkness.

Learning to develop the God in ourselves instead of going after the devil in others is a good way to sort out our projections. Going after the devil in others doesn't give any constructive help to anyone. Making more room in our lives for God and the angels to work will give our minds the creativity we need to deal with the shadow of our lower self. You will naturally follow paths to your higher self, which in turn transforms aspects in the lower self.

Constructively dealing with anger and hate is not an easy process because it takes a conscious effort and much practice. Repressing it does more harm to us and others around us, so we need to open the closet door and free our monster by a constant practice of self-acceptance and developing kindness and wisdom through our spiritual quests. Even the Dalai Lama readily admits it took him much practice to overcome a tendency to get very angry. To quote him: "If you usually remain angry for ten minutes, try to reduce it to eight. Next week make it five minutes and the next month two. Then make it zero. That is how to develop and train our minds. This is my feeling and also the sort of practice I myself do. It is quite clear that everyone needs peace of mind. The question, then, is how to achieve it. Through anger we cannot; through kindness, through love, through compassion, we can achieve one individual's peace of mind." I will return to the theme of anger and self-forgiveness in Chapter 13.

Practice 2: Confronting Fear and Weakness

Now let's look at what our dark side or shadow represents and consists of. Open your mind and bring your angels around; you will want them with you when you view the shadows. Get your journal out or a pen and paper, because you are going to make a list of your negative traits, imperfections, general weaknesses, and human frailties. On one side of the paper, list a trait you have trouble with; for example, you might list jealousy, shame, envy, greed, cruelty, misdirected anger, judgment of self and others, or anything else that presents itself as a struggle in your personality. Now, on the other side of the paper, write about the source of the trait, the way it presents itself as a struggle, and its origin; then figure out what it is defending you against. In other words, define the trait in terms of a fear you have and try to trace it to a concrete example in your life. My guess is that almost everything we hide in our shadows is a result of a childhood fear or adult fear developed from relationships and basic dealings in a scary world. After you have examined the trait and the fear, fantasize ways to eliminate it and write down the positive antidote to the negative trait. Be sure to ask the angels to join you in this transformation. As an example, here's a scenario concerning the trait of jealousy. Look for the source of jealousy in your life, and then imagine what your worst fear is concerning this emotion. After you have done this, realize one essential fact: You have this fear in your mind right now, and you can develop constructive ways to eliminate the problem through practice and by truthfully acknowledging the times it wants to take over.

Make a separate list of positive qualities and light qualities you possess. Now think of a trait from your light side list that may help you overcome the fear involved with the negative trait you want to transform. Ask the angels to remind you with inspiration each time a negative trait arises, so that you can follow it to its source (fear) and choose to abolish it.

Fear is a creativity and happiness killer; allowing fear to have power in our lives by not acknowledging it can lead to negative outcomes such as depression, serious illness, and feeling trapped in unhappy relationships. These negative outcomes are warning signals that we are past due on increasing self-love and self-acceptance — a sign to get back on our path and develop our true, special gift of love. The angels are with us, and they do not look for or reward perfection. They reward self-honesty, and they do this by guiding us to be strong inside and to develop mental peace and happiness without reason, so that in turn we will cast a delightful glow on the world around us.

Practice 3: Listing Ways You Cheat Yourself

Life is really a series of choices. Every day, we are confronted by choices and decisions — large and small, life threatening or life enhancing. Each of us is where we are because of these choices and decisions. Sometimes we feel powerless over our choices — for example, when we are addicted to (or dependent on) something. We make a choice each time we engage in an addictive or habitual action. The key is to be aware of the moment of choice and fight the urge to take the easy way out.

Wanting it easy is a way we cheat ourselves and get into trouble. This may involve telling a little lie when telling the truth seems more difficult. Or maybe we choose to have a drink when we are nervous instead of using our inner resources to overcome the nervousness. Whatever the specifics, following a pattern of taking what we think to be an easy way out hinders spiritual growth. Looking for the easy way out can become habit forming, and before long it spreads into too many areas of our lives, taking us farther away from our spiritual goals and practices.

Take a piece of paper, or get out your journal, and make a list on one side of the paper including the following words: health, prosperity, love/romance, spirituality, relationships, honest communication, career, creativity, parenting, compassion, and positive thinking (along with any other issues you can think of that make up your life). Now, on the opposite side of the paper, list how you may be cheating in any way regarding the particular issue and might therefore be sabotaging your progress and happiness. After you do this, take a moment and call in your angels for some education time. Check to see if you are being too hard on yourself, too critical or unforgiving, and focus on creating an accurate picture of blocks that may exist from a source of avoidance. Forgive yourself and ask the angels to give you some insight for changing and working against the natural force of wanting it easy. The angels will help you see that sometimes the easy way out is actually more work in the long run. If you start practicing responsible action and stick with it, the tendency to cheat will lose its grip on you. You will be on your way, and your path will take a turn upward, heading straight toward the divine light.

Part Two

Empowerment Through
Positive Thinking

About Part Two:

Angels as Guardians of the Positive

Empowerment gives us authority in life—the authority to choose our own way of being. First, we need self-awareness and an honest view of ourselves. This section focuses on eliminating the negative programs in our minds that sabotage our success in life. Before positive thinking can empower us, we need to eliminate negative thinking. Negative thoughts do negative things in our lives such as depress our vitality and suppress our immune systems; influence other people around us negatively; bias our perceptions in favor of detecting and focusing on the negative aspects of existence and therefore make us expect or unconsciously search for negative results to confirm our negative expectations; and cause us to waste positive time.

Positive thoughts do the exact opposite, but first we need room in our minds for them. Positive thinking is a way to use our imagination or visualizing powers to create a successful future. Sometimes we need help from above to sustain the positive thoughts we have and to help us eliminate the negative thoughts. Angels are always ready and willing to encourage the positive. They will give us clues for actions we need to take and ways to make our lives easier and more successful. To have the true power of creative visualization and positive thinking, we need the angels; this section describes ways to combine forces with the angels for true empowerment. Empowerment means the angels are cheering us on, inspiring us, awakening our enthusiasm, bringing glad tidings, affirming our self-worth, and loving us to the point of exhilaration.

When taken at face value, the messages and techniques offered in this book are not new. Basically, all of the information I offer in this book encourages a form of positive thinking meant to inspire spiritual growth. But in contrast to many writers on positive thinking, I stress the ways angels can help us with all our positive changes and spiritual growth, for angels are truly the guardians of positive thinking.

In the past twenty years, I have read many books that have inspired me and made sense to me while I read them, but soon thereafter the inspiration wore off and the techniques I had started to incorporate fell by the wayside. Then one day I read the quotation "Angels can fly because they take themselves lightly" by G. K. Chesterton, and my life changed. This quotation had such a strong impact for two reasons: First, I realized I was taking myself and my spiritual quest far too seriously, and, second, I realized that angels were the missing link in the chain of positive-thinking books and spiritual self-help books that I had been reading. Now, even though I fall short at times and have a negative thought, I don't take it seriously. With the help of the angels, I become aware of what I am creating at each moment, which enables me to choose my course. Now, whenever I read a book that is inspiring, awakening, and full of divine intelligence, the experience is much more rewarding because I can incorporate angel help and inspiration into the messages and they remain longer in my brain, truly helping to make changes in my consciousness.

Another important lesson I have learned is that in order for positive thoughts to thrive in our minds so we can make true changes, we must eliminate the negative beliefs that compete with positive thoughts. There is a very fine line between the reality of positive thinking and the idea of it. For some people, positive thinking remains a good intention, but for others it becomes a way of life, a real way to create a positive self-image and personal happiness by correcting negative thought programs. In the angelic realm, thoughts are the same as actions. The thoughts we hold in our minds at any given moment appear as forms to the angels. Because the angels have direct access to our minds if we want them to, they can help lift our spirits and direct our thoughts to a higher spiritual level.

Our guardian angels are connected with our survival instinct. They are with us all the time, and they can perform miracles when our lives are threatened, as long as our survival program is positive and thriving. In the cases of people who have a death wish and really want to destroy themselves, guardian angels have to step back because they cannot participate in this destructive program; they can only return if the life-affirming force resurfaces and the people change their minds and ask for help. Be assured that your guardian angel is always waiting (right behind you) for the chance to take part in your positive choices.

Our guardian angels protect us by keeping our brain positively programmed to be life affirming so we can enjoy ourselves. This is a constant battle for the angels because our minds are influenced so easily and too often we hear messages that work against the positive. It is astonishing how many negative messages children hear each day. Such messages can range from the outright horrible, where children are actually told they are bad, evil, stupid, and ugly, to something less obvious. From the beginning, most of us have had people in our lives who set out to break our spirit, to tame and control us. I ask the children I work with how often they are told how well they did something, how free spirited they are, and how great and unique and loved they are. Too often I learn that the positive messages are few and far between. Instead, they are told: "Do it this way. Can't you do anything right? Are you stupid or something? That is so bad. Do that again and you will be punished. Wash your face; it's filthy." They hear these messages from people who heard the same messages in their own childhoods, messages intended to break the human spirit and fit it into some concept of acceptable behavior. These negative messages disconnect us from our inner child, and for an obvious reason—survival.

My point here is that every human on this planet has heard negative messages. Over time, we develop negative programs that automatically play back to us when we are about to do something great with our lives. If we can transcend the negative, we can become more self-reliant and overcome hardships by turning them into positive growth experiences. If we eliminate negative, life-defeating programs, we will have the courage to be who we really are and offer our gifts to the world as whole beings, reconnected with the child within us—our pure, creative, and life-affirming force.

Chapter 5

Eliminating Negative Programs and Patterns

Again and again I have emphasized that the process of spiritual growth is an effortful and difficult one. This is because it is conducted against a natural resistance, against a natural inclination to keep things the way they were, to cling to the old maps and old ways of doing things, to take the easy path.
M. Scott Peck, The Road Less Traveled

We are what we think. Thoughts create our state of mind, which in turn creates our present experience. Our present experience can be happy or sad depending on the thoughts in our minds. Having happy thoughts most of the time make us happy; having sad thoughts most of the time make us sad. Having angry thoughts make us angry. Kind thoughts make us compassionate and sweet. Greedy thoughts make us jealous and envious. Loving thoughts make us lovers. The predominant type of thought creates a corresponding state of mind. These states of mind also affect our body language and even our physiology. When we are angry or worried, our stomachs start to churn from the excess acid released in response to the emotion. The effects of our thinking go beyond our brains into our bodies.

Whatever we practice repeatedly becomes ingrained into behavior patterns, and too many of us practice negative instead of positive thinking. Imagine that your mind works like a computer. The brain corresponds to the computer itself, and the mind to the programs that are fed to the computer. In this way, negative thoughts (input) become negative programs that result in negative behavior (output)—bad habits, bad luck, bad health, and so forth. Repetitive patterns are difficult to eliminate. Negative thoughts resulting in negative behavior patterns are constant setbacks on the path to bliss and happiness. Negative behavior patterns need to be detected, edited, reprogrammed, and eliminated in order for positive patterns to surface and bring us happiness and prosperity.

At one time or another, you may have tried to tap into the power of positive thinking. Many people have considered positive thinking to be the key to solving all our problems and helping us live happily ever after. We are supposed to be able to create heaven here on earth simply by visualizing and thinking wonderful, positive thoughts. The trouble is that unless we eliminate the negative programs from our thinking process, the true benefits of positive thinking cannot find a way through the negative patterns. If you have tried using the power of positive thinking and have given up, all is not lost. Positive thinking will work for you if you increase your self-esteem by getting rid of the programs in your mind that tell you "I am not good enough" or "I am not deserving of happiness" and if you recognize the angels as natural guardians of the positive in your own brain.

When we were born, our minds were programmed to create happiness and love. Our natural drive, the first program we were sent to earth with, is life affirming. We are meant to evolve and expand our true inner nature. That first program still exists within our minds. Deeply ingrained in our soul, it is our true connection to the angelic realm. If we are all born so capable of living a happy existence, why is it that so many of us don't? There are as many answers to this question as there are unhappy humans on this planet. From birth, we learn to react to the world around us from people who have influence over us and from the experience of our unique position in the world. We have all adopted patterns and programs, some negative and some positive, that fit our experiences of life.

The negative programs we learn as we grow up interfere with the original positive program, while positive programs nourish and expand it. Detecting and eliminating negative patterns and programs will allow us to get that first program back so we can function as innocently as we did the first day we took a breath of air. All the pure sweet thoughts of heaven the angels sent us to earth with are still available to us.

Practice 1: Brain Program Editors

Have you ever considered why a bad habit is so difficult to eliminate? And why is it so difficult to change our way of thinking? Why can't alcoholics just stop drinking when they want to and why can't smokers just stop smoking? These questions are baffling. In *Quantum Healing*, Deepak Chopra helps explain why habits and addictions are so difficult to eliminate. Because memory is more permanent than matter, a cell's memory is able to outlive the cell itself. According to Chopra, "If you take an addict, detoxify his body, and keep him away from alcohol or drugs for several years, all the old cells that used to be 'chemically addicted' are totally gone. Yet the memory persists, and if you give it a chance the memory will latch onto the addictive substance once again."

Addicts in the recovery process know exactly how powerful memory can be. For people who have been addicted to a drug, just passing by the house or neighborhood where they got high can be a serious threat to their sobriety. Time away can help heal this phenomenon, but only if the time away consists of conscious inner strengthening work (prayer, self-honesty, meditation, and so forth). I once heard an alcoholic who had been sober for seven years talk about how it wasn't any easier after all these years to face life sober. The problem is that the only change he made was to stop drinking, to discontinue the act of raising the glass to his mouth. Freeing yourself of negative patterns won't get easier unless you do the inner work and make changes in the thinking that caused the problem in the first place. Doing the inner work with the angels at your side will prove that life can get easier and that time does heal!

A similar example concerns grief and the holidays or seasons of the year. The level of the sun in the sky, casting shadows in a particular way, can trigger feelings from years past. Smells in the air can remind us of people, places, and times. Hearing favorite or not-so-favorite songs also evokes memories. The memories of a certain habit or way of doing things are also strong and very resistant to change. We have free will, so we don't have to allow a habit or brain program to run its course, but we must make a conscious effort to stop it. And to change our behaviors for the future, we need to reprogram and upgrade our computer-mind so a different program will run. The brain program editing angels can help edit out unwanted behavior programs.

Brain program editors are tiny angels of light that have access to cells and neurotransmitters if we allow them to. They can help us transform negative beliefs to positive ones and "addicted" cells to free cells. To allow this transformation to take place, we must know deep inside that all things are possible, then pray and ask the angels to sustain our faith in a positive outcome. To keep our faith in transformation strong means taking our cues and doing our part in following through with changes. Miraculous healings of the negative are possible, but first the stage must be set and then we must follow through.

With the angel brain program editors, we can set up alarms and detectors for the onset of negative programs, thoughts, or feelings so we can change perspectives instantly before the negative trend takes hold. When the alarm system is working, a little voice will click in and tell you when you start being negative about something. You may experience this voice as a clear thought coming through in the middle of something else, asking you, "Do you really want to be this negative?" After your first warning, you will have the choice to either continue on the negative course or change by admitting you are being negative and stopping. If you choose not to stop, in a few moments another alarm will go off and again you will have the choice to stop and change perspectives. I know by experience that it isn't always easy to use these choices wisely, but as time goes on and you practice it gets a lot easier. At the very least, the alarm system brings you much greater self-awareness regardless of what you choose. To set the alarm system and negative detectors, ask the brain program editors to install them and then declare that you will be willing to do the actual work of shifting gears when you want to end a negative behavior, belief, or thought. An interesting thing happens when you continue being negative with full awareness of it: You begin to notice the way the people around you react and the way negative events follow. Seeing this in living color usually gives you the motivation to quit.

As M. Scott Peck suggested in the opening quotation, the main reason change is so difficult is that the process of change is conducted against a natural resistance, an inclination to keep things the way they are. If we change our habits and our thinking, we may fear that our marriage will fall apart, or our job will feel less satisfying, or our friends won't understand us, and so on. Keep in mind, these fears only exist in our minds. While these things might happen, they might not, and if they do it usually means positive changes and happiness are coming our way. If we make a negative statement such as "Well, I'm not even going to try to get that job because they only hire family members or friends who aren't really talented," this only means we are fearful of what may happen if we put our talent on the line.

Maybe the statement about the job is true only because they haven't found talent such as ours. When you make a negative statement, examine where it is coming from: Is it coming from a space of fear or a space of anger? Get your journal out and think of a negative belief, then write down a positive affirmation that will replace the negative, bringing the angels in to help you believe the positive affirmation and transform the negative belief.

The key here is having faith; don't make problems for yourself before they happen! Have faith that with the angels around you, you can transform any problem for the highest good of all concerned. The brain program editors are at your service, so if you want to change and grow, there aren't any excuses!

Practice 2: Declarations of Change

The written word has a power of its own, especially when the angels are involved. So if you need help with changing a thought pattern or bad habit, get out a piece of paper and start writing. Make a declaration of independence from negative beliefs, stale patterns, and old maps. Announce formally that you willingly and happily accept change, and declare that new patterns with positive outcomes replace the negative and stale old ways. Do this in whatever way works for you, and be creative with it. Declare all your faults, all your excess baggage, and then be willing to give them up for the good of your higher self. Have fun and bring in some humor to change your perspective. Human beings are delightfully funny when they laugh at themselves and enjoy the craziness of human existence. Formally announce your faith in the angels; they will help you get through the low times, but most importantly they will help you allow yourself to be happy and accept the fact that you deserve some true mental peace and well-being. You are a wonderful, valuable human being whose life is a light unto the earth, and the angels want you to enjoy that fact. Go, team, go! Take the ball and run!

Practice 3: Smiling to Erase Negative Programs

There are no language barriers when you are smiling. That smile on your face is a light to tell people that your heart is at home.

Allen Klein

Just as memory in the cells can trigger negative feelings, a memory can also trigger positive feelings. Smiling is an example of this. You smile naturally at those moments when you are happy or about to laugh, so it figures that moving your mouth into a smile will trigger a happy response. Use your smile as an eraser for negative thoughts. When a negative thought pops up, smile it away. Let yourself feel the process of your smile erasing negative feelings out of your mind, or visualize your smile as a splash of water that washes away the negative.

I think of a smile as a beautiful light shining through a person's face. When people smile, they look beautiful regardless of physical features; the angels promote beauty on this earth, and they love a good smile. When we smile, we attract angel energy.

I know there are many times when we just don't feel like smiling, and I can't stand it when someone tells me to smile with complete disregard for other elements of the situation. But you can tell yourself to smile even when you don't feel like it, and smiling just may change your mood and attitude. In other words, smile anyway, because the action of smiling will attract angels to you and the angels will help you erase the negative and transform your perception to the positive.

When you aren't smiling and don't feel like it, try to identify the reason. Look in the mirror and notice what your expression tells you. Maybe you're bored and have a blank, apathetic look on your face. Or maybe you're worried about something and have a concerned or tormented look. Do you look sad and unhappy? Angry? Mean? Perplexed? Take a look and observe without judging, follow your expression to its source, and then start to smile. Whether it feels genuine or not, do it. And if you are someone who smiles all the time, even when you are upset, don't change; just look at what that means, without making a negative judgment about yourself.

Here are some things to remember about smiling: It is difficult to be rude or mean to someone smiling, so if you smile more the rest of the world will treat you better. A smile attracts angels, so if you feel fear in a situation, smile and your protection will increase. Smiling gets easier with practice. When a full-fledged smile comes over you, the happiness and peace of the angels surround and engulf you.

Chapter 6

Incorporating Positive Abundance Thinking

But now and then, somehow, through a grace beyond comprehension, we break out of this self-perpetuating cycle, touch another dimension of understanding and become filled with a new realization. From that moment of birth we are in a new framework; we can never return to our old view of ourselves and life. Although habitual moulds may tend to obscure that moment of clarity, from then on our problems and challenges assume a different aspect.

Dorothy Maclean

Changing our lives and our characters may not always be easy, but a time comes when circumstances beyond our wildest imagination give us the impetus to change. Just when we think that we are in a rut or that life is boring, depressing, or dysfunctional, something happens to change our way of thinking. We put our priorities in order. If you have gotten into a rut, and feel out of synch with the universe, it is time to bring in the positive thinking force and create a new framework for yourself. The angels always remind us when it is time to get out of a rut. They do this by sending us messages. Maybe someone in our life holds us in very high esteem. Maybe someone sees the rut we are in and tries to relay messages from the angels about how wonderful we are. Maybe a child sees our true essence and reminds us every once in a while. Maybe messages appear in movies we watch or books we read. The angels have many ways of gently nudging us back on track, and they can be very subtle, so we have to pay close attention. Just know they are there—the happiness trainers ready to participate in turning us toward the magic of a happy reality, the prosperity brokers never letting up on lessons of abundance, the creativity ministers and muses ready to guide us to our artistic nature and bring us creative freedom. To receive all the gifts the angels are waiting to give, we must incorporate positive programs and patterns back into our lives, because angels can only participate in the positive.

When the negative is out of the way, the positive naturally thrives. We can use angelic connections to help us program abundance and prosperity. The angels can go into our brain and plant the seeds of new projects and ideas that will germinate and grow to fruition. We can program lightness, happiness, bliss—anything our heart desires—and the angels will encourage and enlighten our way. It is important to trust the angels and not try to figure out logically what they are doing or put limits on what they can do in our lives by being too rational. When I share angel experiences I hear with other people, some people immediately try to figure out a logical explanation to take credit away from angels, or they say, "That couldn't happen." Well, with that kind of thinking, it couldn't possibly happen in their lives. And if anything wonderful did happen, they might miss it entirely by being too rational.

The universe is full of positive energy systems we can tap into with the angels' help. These energy systems are powerful centers of loving light vibrations; using visualization practices, we can connect with them and tap the power. The energy system of beauty is medicine for the soul; tap into this system by bringing beauty into your life, by surrounding yourself with fresh flowers or visiting beautiful places such as city gardens. Peace is also an energy system; it has a calming effect on your nervous system and brings clarity to the mind. Healing light is an energy system available to heal our body/mind. Enthusiasm is also an energy system; enthusiasm is inspiration lit up with fire in our souls. It enables us to have perseverance and to approach life with an energy that says, "I will succeed and I will not take no as an answer." Having enthusiasm doesn't mean being reckless or impatient; when you tap into the true essence of enthusiasm, it teaches you to walk each step of the way and create life as a gift. In the words of Ralph Waldo Emerson, "Nothing great was ever achieved without enthusiasm." And don't ever forget the energy system of humor, which is so important to every aspect of our being. Humor can truly make us superhuman, because it releases us from the gravity of this world and its heavy, serious problems.

Money is a recurring issue in most of our lives. We need money to live, and it possesses energy because it provides the basics for our survival. Having food, shelter, and clothing depends on having money; we can lose our creative sight by worrying all the time about how to provide for ourselves. To remain creative and free from worry, we must tap into the abundance energy system and start to educate ourselves about prosperity. Abundance creates its own energy system in the universe consisting of angelic gifts and bonuses for your life. By tapping into this system, you will feel you have more than enough to make your life exciting and worth living. Gifts from the abundance system originate from the kingdom of God and may not manifest as simply as you would like, meaning you may not get a check in the mail if you ask for money but you may get an idea of how to convert your talents and time into more negotiable commodities. If you do ask for a check or money in its physical form, of course you may receive it, but I just want you to be prepared if it doesn't come. Nevertheless, I heard two people in one day tell me that their angel prosperity brokers had solved their problems with cold, hard cash. I was guiding a workshop in Seattle at the Body, Mind, and Spirit Expo, and was blessed with the presence of three women who call themselves A.I.T.s (Angels in Training). Their foundation was once running very low on cash, and they needed a certain amount of it right away. They asked for this amount, wondering how "on earth" they would get it. Then, one of the women was driving along a country road and twenty-dollar bills began falling out of the sky. Another person also noticed this, and both of them pulled over, looked in the sky, and saw nothing visible that could be dumping this money down to earth. The other driver suggested they start collecting the bills. It turned out that the cash collected was exactly enough to bail the A.I.T.s out of their particular situation, and nothing ever explained the phenomenon, such as a bank robbery, so the money was meant for them. Another participant at the workshop told me afterward that he had wanted to attend the workshop but didn't have the extra twenty dollars needed. He paid to get into the expo and reached in his pocket and found an extra twenty-dollar bill. This was a true surprise to him, because as a student he kept close track of his money. He spent the twenty dollars on the workshop, then heard the synchronistic story of the twenty-dollar bills, which made him realize that the angels had somehow given him what he needed.

The student's experience reminded me of a time when I wasn't working and had very little cash, but it seemed as though my wallet always had money in it. In fact, my friend noticed this and exclaimed that money was creating itself in my wallet! But I have also experienced times when the money itself has not manifested in my wallet, and these times have been true tests of faith and ingenuity. As I continue to struggle with the lessons of abundance, I must say the lessons and trials themselves are more valuable to me than any twenty-dollar bill or store-bought item ever will be. Creating wealth is actually more fun than having it at times. I once knew a person who had been a millionaire five times, and each time lost it all. I think he lost it on purpose. Granted, this man was a bit eccentric, but he had more fun creating wealth than being a millionaire.

If you already have a certain amount of wealth, the abundance network of angels, the prosperity brokers, will want to teach you how to enjoy it more with love. Basically, the angels want to instill the attitude that our life force is its own fortune, a true gift from the kingdom of God regardless of status. Money and wealth are volatile issues in all of our lives, regardless of how much we have or don't have. Money can be a curse or a blessing; it all depends on our attitude. So tap into the abundance system and be ready to test your faith and sense of humor, but always remember the prosperity brokers are there for you and if you fall they will catch you, one way or another.

Practice 1: Developing Angelic Visualization Techniques

When you expect the best, you release a magnetic force in your mind which by law of attraction tends to bring the best to you.
    Norman Vincent Peale, The Power of Positive Thinking

In Chapter 5, we talked about the angel brain program editors; for this exercise, we want to use the angel positive thinking programmers. Once we have made conscious efforts to edit and remove our negative programs, it is time to incorporate new programs and create a positive future.

Many people have written about our capacity to create the future through manifestation, with techniques ranging from intellectual planning to creative visualization. The power of the focused mind to make external events fall into place often seems extraordinary. There are several levels of explanation for how this works, and when it works. On one level of explanation, we are simply ordering our minds to be prepared to say and do the right things at the right times, consistent with achieving what we want. On the next level, we consider the possibility that our ideal thought or image influences others psychically, even drawing to us the right people. Next, we consider that our ideal images are communicated to an ordering intelligence — God and the angels — that can arrange fortuitous coincidences. This may sound like the traditional concept of a wish granted or a prayer answered; however, the most effective method is not to ask for something in the future, but rather to "dream" it as ideally present in the here and now.

Imagine an ideal situation, draw the pieces of the ideal around yourself in the present, and allow the details and ramifications to fall into place and elaborate themselves to complete your image. Use vivid mental experiences and take the time and effort required to complete them. Visualization is much more than simply thinking about something; it is more like a dream where you have all the sensory experiences of waking life, meaning you can smell, taste, hear, touch, and see what you're visualizing, and your body may react physiologically by a changing heart rate and so on. All visualization exercises need to be practiced and the images deeply ingrained in your mind so you can readily access them when needed. Think of areas in your life where you can visualize success. Athletes often use visualization to become their personal best. If you are dieting or changing bad habits, visualize your progress. If you have a project that needs help, visualize the outcome you want. The most important aspect of visualization is that it requires you to focus your energy and define your goals and discover specific steps required to complete it. Vague goals and indefinite plans won't work with the true art of visualization. The act of visualization is a form of programming your brain. If you find the future brings new needs, update the visualization. A visualization is open to change and expansion; as you grow, you will discover new avenues of success you would like to program. So don't worry about change;

it is important and vital at times, and it can bring new life to your goals.

Now energize your ideal visualization with feeling. Ask the angels, the cosmic network, to watch over your visualized ideal and hold it in a sacred space in a savings account in your imagination. Whenever needed, open the savings account and add more or take what is needed at the time. Develop angelic visualization techniques for your highest good, and that of the universe. These techniques are worth incorporating in all of your spiritual practices, and they are especially helpful for tapping into the loving and positive energy systems in the universe.

Practice 2: Planting Your Angelic Mind Garden

One way to incorporate positive programs is to visualize your life as a garden. Some lives look like beautiful English gardens, with the colors all blending together as in an impressionist painting. Other life gardens may be full of wildflowers, with tall trees representing strength in one area. Some may be very well manicured and in perfect order, never inviting child's play or a casual pick of a bouquet. Sadly, some lives may look like unkempt gardens with weeds, browning plants, and barren trees, but there's no need to despair even in this case, because a garden can always be replanted and weeded.

Think about your own garden. If you like, get out a piece of paper and draw a picture of it. Use your imagination and have fun. New projects may appear as seedlings; a tree may represent one's family; a rose bush, love and romance; flowering vines, friendships; and so forth. Now, after you have your mind garden clearly visualized, be the gardener and look around at what needs to be done. Perhaps there is an overgrown area that needs trimming, or some weeds that need removing so you can plant some new seeds. If the garden looks pretty good, think of some areas you would like to harvest or cultivate. Think of ways to increase healthy growth (fertilizer), and keep these in your mind. Think of some of the fruits of your labor that may be ready for harvest. If the garden is overgrown and out of control, plan on doing some weeding and cultivating. Whatever the state of your garden, leave some room to plant new seeds, and some room for the angels to play with. They may want to introduce you to a new strain of flower or fruit, but they need the space.

Now go into angel alpha state, and visualize your mind garden. Think about the seeds you would like to plant and visualize how they will look as they grow and flourish. Clear a space and allow the angels to go into your mind and plant the seed. Ask the angels to watch over the seedlings and allow their growth to be strong and healthy. Ask the angels for insight into how to make your garden grow. Ask if there are hidden weeds, or if a weed could actually become a beautiful wildflower. Are there branches in the way? Is one plant crowding out another?

After you have visualized and enjoyed your garden for a while, stay in angel alpha state and quiet your mind. Now ask the angels for some seed thoughts. Seed thoughts are ideas that you may choose to grow in the future. Seed thoughts need time to germinate in your mind through meditation. A seed thought may mean the start of the biggest project you will ever undertake, or it may be an idea you play with in your meditations for years, until it develops into a belief or concept. Remember you are the gardener and, with the angels at your side, you can make your garden as big and as beautiful as you want.

Practice 3: Changing Perceptions in an Instant

A perception is an immediate or intuitive feeling or judgment we have, a simple awareness or observation based on contact with our senses. To truly encourage change, we must be able to release our perceptions and allow new ones to form based on new and more accurate information. In other words, sometimes we must step out of our own way and allow the angels to give us a new view of a situation. Our perceptions form very quickly, usually before we have time to think about or weigh the situation thoroughly. So our perceptions can be clouded by lots of personal and emotional feelings or moods. When we can release ourselves from our perceptions, and keep them free and mutable, the angels have more room to keep the avenues of positive thinking open. Clear intuition and emotional perceptions are different; the first is a much more accurate sizing of a situation or person. Think about perceptions and intuition in your own life and ways you may have gotten stuck in the past. The angels are keepers of the positive flame of thought, and if you stay open they can give you a new take on any situation. Angels remain true to the issue at hand, and new perceptions gained with their help are positive and encourage positive outcomes. It can all happen in an instant.

Chapter 7

Imagination as Your Direct Line to the Kingdom

Angels are creatures of imagination. This does not mean they are any less real than you are. As Shakespeare said, "We are such stuff as dreams are made of." And angels are evidently made of the same stuff as the nonmaterial aspect of ourselves. Angels can coexist with us in our individual worlds of ideas, thoughts, and images.

Francis Jeffrey

Many people try to negate the existence of angels by saying angels are just part of our imagination. But what is our imagination? I could not possibly believe that there is nothing beyond the human brain, and at the same time believe that my mind is expanded. These beliefs cancel each other out. I personally believe that the body/brain and the physical world are only half of the big picture. Imagination is our link to the other half.

Why even try to define imagination? Just allow it to be; defining always imposes limits. Having a vivid imagination is so much fun that I wouldn't want to limit it or confine it with boundaries, rules, or pointless descriptions. We have to accept the fact that there are certain mysteries in life, especially in the spiritual sense. And maybe the source of imagination is one of these mysteries. We all have imagination, and the more intimate we become with the powers of our imagination, the better we will understand ourselves and our powers of creation.

I bought a book once I was sure I would love because it was about living happily and creating joy and luck and all sorts of wonderful things that I love to write and talk about. As I read the book, I began to get turned off because it kept referring to "creative people," as if they were an elite class of humans. I kept reading about how "creative people" do this and "creative people" do that. Even "creative people" have a hard time recognizing themselves in this book! The author was judging only certain achievements and personality traits as creative, and setting up a barrier to creativity for people who might not hold these particular traits. I believe that we are all creative in our own ways, and that judging certain things as creative and others as not is very limiting.

Certain components of creativity may inhibit some people from exploring their own creative nature. First of all, creativity requires a certain amount of courage. Rollo May wrote a wonderful book on creativity entitled *The Courage to Create*. In it, he writes, "Courage is not a virtue or a value among other personal values like love or fidelity. It is the foundation that underlies and gives reality to all other virtues and personal values. The word *courage* comes from the same stem as the French word *coeur*, meaning 'heart.' Thus just as one's heart, by pumping blood to one's arms, legs, and brain enables all the other physical organs to function, so courage makes possible all the psychological virtues."

One reason it takes courage to be creative is that you may end up discovering new ways of doing things or new ways of being that threaten other people's comfort with the old ways, or your creative discovery may challenge an idea people aren't ready to let go of. So being creative doesn't necessarily go hand in hand with being popular. And it may mean breaking a couple of rules.

Creativity implies production, so there must be an encounter or action to bring something into existence. To be creative, you must do something about it, follow through with your ideas, allow yourself to take a risk or two, and cultivate freedom of expression. Some people have never had a safe place to explore their own brand of creative ideas. Therefore, they may fear following through with their ideas. The critic, the censorship committee, and the "cool police" are always right around the corner ready to judge, ready to tell us what is okay to do and what isn't. Rejection and criticism are lethal to creative energy, and there are too many critics on this planet right now. Hang in there; this is where the angels can be of great help. The angels are anticriticism; anything that will help you feel good about yourself and bring you into alignment with your highest self is praiseworthy to them, and they are your best cheerleaders. Ask them to hold the critics at bay while you are in a creative space, to protect your own creativity as a fragile and precious possession.

Have you ever had an idea just pop into your mind? You have probably had the experience of saying, "It just dawned on me" or "It came to me in a daydream." Well, those were probably the times your personal angel creativity minister called on you. Many poets past and present acknowledge their personal muses who bring them inspiration. These experiences of inspiration can be cultivated. First, pay attention to their timing. Are you driving your car and letting your mind wander when creative ideas come to you? Are you doing some routine activity such as washing dishes or shaving, or dozing off into sleep? Many people who have had earthshaking ideas say that the ideas came to them at times when they weren't trying to think but were engaged in a routine activity. The first time I had the idea to write *Messengers of Light* was when I was just kidding around with a friend and said, "I can never find the type of angel book I want to read; I should write a book." Believe me, writing it required all the components of creativity I have mentioned: I had to muster up courage and keep it with me, fighting my own doubts and those of others. And the process didn't make me too popular with people who have been writing for years; some of them kept trying to make the process more difficult for me because they had certain beliefs about writing books that didn't go along with my writing one. But I stuck with it, and the book found its way to the best publisher for that type of book, and, thanks to several loving people (my human cheerleaders) who were open-minded, the book became reality, and a successful one at that. Also, I received built-in inspiration from my angel creativity ministers, since the subject matter was close to their hearts.

A creative encounter awaits you; if you have found it, bring in the angels to enhance and expand it. If you have yet to discover where your creativity lies, allow the angels to show you.

Practice 1: Using Your Imagination

This world is but canvas to our imaginations. Dreams are the touchstones of our characters.

                                        Henry David Thoreau

Your imagination is the only place where the future exists, so if you want to create a wonderful future you must get used to doing so by using your imagination. I personally believe that our imagination is our direct line to God and the angels. It is our secret place where we can talk to invisible friends (angels) and think up wonderful fantasies about heaven. It is a safe place where we can be anything we want to be.

Small children are usually encouraged to let their imaginations run wild. Then, when they come up with stuff that is too much for the adults around them, they are admonished to stop. I know that these days more and more people honor the imagination, but most of us at some point were told, "That's just your imagination," which stopped us from letting our imaginations go. So some of us may need to retrain our imagination to run wild again. To do this, we have to use our imagination and come up with ways to explore its hidden corners. You may want to start by going into angel alpha state and asking the angels to guide you on a tour of your own imagination. What you find there will be unique; all I can do is encourage you to go within and wish you *bon voyage!*

Practice 2: *Accessing Your Muse*

Love is an energy pattern available for our creativity. Many people are discovering this fun fact and tapping into this energy to give their own brand of love to the world. The universe holds many gifts and treasures available to us through our imagination. One way to get to these gifts and treasures is by connecting with our personal angel muses and guides. A muse is an angel of creative inspiration. There are muses for all the various expressions of art, music, craft, writing, and so forth — specific angels who hold the expansion keys offered to humans when they bypass the ordinary. As with any angelic intervention, accessing your muse occurs through inspiration, and only if and when you ask for it; this process by no means takes away from your own unique creative talents.

Think of your muse as the keeper of your blueprint or vision. Your creative muse gives you access to a special research department, where all sorts of new ideas and gifts you can develop await to be discovered. So if you are not yet sure what you are doing here, get in touch with your muse and together come up with an idea. If you are sure about what you are doing, get in touch with your muse to encourage, inspire, and guide you to greatness. Remember, the world stands back to let those who know where they are going pass by. Know where you are going, take your time getting there, ask the angels of creativity to share your path, and amazing things will happen!

Part Three

Recovery and Wisdom

About Part Three:

Self-Help and the Angels

Self-help: Think about this commonly used term for a moment. When I think of self-help, I think of books I have read and of Twelve-Step programs such as Alcoholics Anonymous (A.A.). I hold the idea of self-help in high esteem. Self-help programs allow us to find help without depending on external sources for that help; they help us tap into spiritual support. Help exists on many levels and can mean many things. When people are drowning, they scream for help, and when people are blocked, they ask for help. Children ask for help a lot because the world is designed for taller people. When I get stuck, I ask my angels for help, then take their cues about what I can do to remedy a situation.

Changing our character changes our destiny. All of us who are reaching upward, all of us who are traveling a spiritual path, all of us who are striving to improve our way of life, to break negative patterns, and to change our character are seeking spiritual help. There are many forms of self-help available, but something that is often overlooked is the role angels can play with self-help. Angels are basically facilitators, which means they make things easier, lessening difficulty and struggle. Even though we all have to figure it out for ourselves in our own ways, the angels are with us. We are not alone. This is where it is up to you to be creative. If you are reading a self-help book, if you are in therapy, or if you are in a Twelve-Step program, call on the angels to support you and your progress will accelerate.

Chapter 8

Angels as Guardians of the Twelve Steps

Twelve-step programs are expanding rapidly as a form of self-help for a vast range of issues. The twelve steps offer a universal spiritual path and follow a natural progression toward growth and expansion. In this chapter, I want to offer those of you who are interested or involved in a Twelve-Step program some ideas of how your own personal guardian angels and angels in general can help and guide you. You will need to be creative. I will offer ideas, but you must take the ideas and sculpt them to suit your own path. Also, from the start I want to make it clear that the angels will not do any of the steps for you; in other words, you cannot use them as an excuse to avoid working the steps. Whenever I have tried to bypass one of life's lessons by using the angels to create shortcuts, they have made sure I learned the lessons myself! I also want to make it clear that the angels don't take the place of regularly attending meetings or working with a human sponsor; they are supplements to, not substitutes for, working your program.

Angels offer valuable support because from their viewpoint they see many things we miss here on earth. And they know who you are — in other words, they hold an image of you in your best and highest light — and they are always guiding you (if you want them to) toward this highest light. When we get into troublesome situations, the angels view this as a temporary entanglement. Imagine you are walking along your path of life and a net drops on you from above. You begin to struggle to get free, not understanding what it is that has trapped you. The view from the ground is scary when we get entangled in a trap, but from the angels' view it is very different. They can see that if you just relaxed and figured out what was going on, step by step you could get free of the net. And if you ask for their guidance, you will disentangle yourself faster, because angels have a clearer view of the situation, one that is light as opposed to dark and heavy. And from their view, you would have to admit that the situation may even seem funny. Angels think that we are hilarious, but they are not making fun of us — they love us. One time my niece got stuck in a seat at a movie theater. She wasn't hurt, but she was panicked and was yelling for someone to get her out. From our viewpoint, this was funny and when we got her out she thought so, too. We weren't laughing at her, and the angels won't laugh at us either. It just looks funny from their point of view and this is an advantage for us. Because eventually, after all is said and done and we are okay, we can look back at our lives with love and humor.

Twelve-Step programs offer us maps to follow to disentangle ourselves from our traps. When we finally realize what is going on, step by step we can free ourselves, and our view of the situation becomes much lighter. The angels can help us with the twelve steps, just as they guide us out of any negative situation. From their point of view, the twelve steps make a lot of sense. Angels are especially pleased with the fact that many people find their way back to their spiritual path through Twelve-Step programs, and begin to lead the happy and successful lives they were meant to live.

There are various interpretations of the twelve steps that originated in Alcoholics Anonymous and that are now used for many
other issues as well. In this chapter, I will list the traditional A.A.
steps, and then offer some angel ideas for personal growth.
(Remember that these steps can be used to work through any
negative pattern, not just alcohol abuse.) As you work the steps,
keep your attitude positive and light; you are in good hands with
the angels by your side. Your angel sponsor/guardian angel can
help reinforce your contact with your human sponsor.

A.A. Step 1

*We admitted that we were powerless over alcohol – that our
lives had become unmanageable.*

Basically this step tells us to wake up and get past denial. As
a defense mechanism, denial in some way changes the programming of our brain, enabling us to block out unwanted, difficult,
or painful truths. Step 1 is a call for us to become aware of misplaced power, and begin to regain serenity by the act of admitting what it is we use most of our energy to deny. I think the
key word here is *unmanageable*. Our lives become unmanageable when we try to control everything around us; at such times,
we are really out of control. A life also becomes unmanageable
when we allow other people or addictive substances to control
areas of our lives. By letting go of a need to control or be controlled, we begin to move toward serenity.

Practice 1: The Angels and Step 1

Get into a relaxed state of mind, and begin to connect with your
guardian angel. Ask your guardian angel for an objective view
from above. That is, you are asking to take a look from outside
yourself so you can see exactly what is out of control in your
life. Denial is a powerful defense mechanism and difficult to

break through because its very nature obscures its presence. Ask your guardian angel to help you discover what you are denying and why. Basically, you are seeking insight from a higher viewpoint. Try to define exactly what you are fighting to deny. The fight is what takes away energy that could be used for managing your life. Then work on surrendering; the fight is over, and angelic help is on the way. You have taken the first step toward releasing yourself from the net that has fallen on you. Begin to get used to the idea that this process is about *your* mental health and happiness. This is about healing you and only you.

The essence of Step 1 is channeling energy into letting go, as opposed to fighting and struggling.

Other Angels to Call On for All of the Steps

Your inner wise angel (see Chapter 9), your spirit guides, and your happiness trainers can all support you as you progress through the twelve steps. Ask these angels to help you look at your life in the light of honesty, without fear. Ask them to remind you that they are with you, and that they are the light that gives you sight (insight). Call on any angel you can think of; they all offer hope and optimism as lanterns on your path.

A.A. Step 2

We came to believe that a power greater than ourselves could restore us to sanity.

This step's key essence is hope. What good does it do to face the light of truth and then get depressed over it? This could be even more dangerous than denial. Step 2 encourages us to begin to cultivate optimism, to know that everything is okay and that we are not alone. The angels are purveyors of hope and are always ready to help us access a greater power.

Practice 2: The Angels and Step 2

Get relaxed, close your eyes, and think about the word *angel*. What images, feelings, sounds, and sensations come to mind? Find a positive image and begin to feel the power of love and protection the angels bring you. Begin to repeat: "I am not alone; the love of the angels is with me at all times." Keep repeating this; let the words change if you want, but keep the feeling positive and light. Open to the light; it is the power greater than us that will restore balance and love in our lives. Begin to really believe, then go past belief and begin to know. Repeat positive affirmations whenever you feel alone, and ask the angels to give you a sign that they are with you. *You are not alone!* If you have a guardian angel prayer card (you can purchase one at a Catholic bookstore or a religious supply store), meditate on the picture and what it means to you.

The essence of Step 2 is that the light of hope is with you; you are not alone.

A.A. Step 3

We made a decision to turn our will and our lives over to the care of God as we understood God.

This step encourages us to turn our lives over to God—or whatever name we give the higher power. We need to find out what God or the higher power means to us. This step basically tells us to let go of the notion that we have to be martyrs or that life is just a series of bad luck. We need to let go and let God and the angels guide us to positive, higher ground. This is the step toward experiencing trust in God as a basis for understanding, a step toward turning our will and our lives over to God for the purpose of finding our true self.

Practice 3: The Angels and Step 3

Very simply, say a prayer and declare that you are turning over your struggles to your higher power and the angels. Ask that the angels always be near to remind you to release the struggle and let go. This will take practice, but the angels are good at reminding you when to let go; you just need to attune to their vibration and pay attention. This is a big step because you are letting go of self-will and asking for spiritual transformation. *True recovery is a spiritual path.* It will be unique to each of us, but it will enable us to find out who we are and how we can transform darkness with our own special light.

The essence of Step 3 is to let go and move toward the lighted path.

A.A. Step 4

We made a searching and fearless moral inventory of ourselves.

Our searching and fearless moral inventory needs to be done in the spirit of humor and honesty, and what better way to achieve this than to call in the angels to keep us from taking ourselves too seriously. Also, the angels provide extra light and the willingness to see what is hiding in the dark areas of our personality, areas where the light hasn't shone for a long time. Angels also love to abolish fear, so they are a great help for this step.

Practice 4: The Angels and Step 4

This could be the first step some people take in figuring out who they really are — not who other people are and what others have done, but who the person in the mirror is at the present moment.

Take a piece of paper or get out your journal. Surround yourself in angel light by calling in your angels (your guardian/sponsor angel and others you want nearby). The light will keep fear away as you look within. (In Chapter 4 I discussed the shadow or dark side; you may want to review that chapter as you deal with this step.) Now start to write about qualities and personality traits that come into your mind. You may find yourself wanting to write about the negative qualities of people who are closest to you. Or if you discover something negative in your personality, you may want to blame someone else for it being there. When this urge happens, write down the quality and begin to own it. For example, if the word *irresponsible* comes into your mind, but you think that irresponsibility is someone else's trait, write it down anyway because it is also yours. Everything you project onto others in some way belongs to you as well. This is the time to start being honest with yourself and to let go of fear and defensiveness. In fact, if you are finding it difficult to deal with this step, start writing the qualities that you find to be negative in other people. Do this quickly; in other words, just brainstorm and write down certain words. Now take a look at these traits and open your mind (with love) to the fact that several of these words describe your own barriers to success. Remember that you called in the angels to help you with this practice whenever fear or denial creeps in; ask them to bring more light in if you are feeling stuck. This practice will go wherever you let it. Simply use it as a temporary gauge to see where you are with yourself, to see how much you feel you have to hide. Awareness brings change. Awareness is all you want to accomplish with this step. The rest will happen in its own time. So don't start making all sorts of judgments about yourself. Just become aware, and ask the angels to keep the light of awareness on in your mind; then you will begin to act on behalf of yourself—from the place of your higher self.

The essence of Step 4 is that character is dynamic; it needs room to shed the negative and expand the positive.

A.A. *Step 5*

We admitted to God, to ourselves, and to another human being the exact nature of our wrongs.

I personally don't like calling things wrong or right because these are simply opinions and we usually cling too tightly to our concepts of right and wrong. But there is something very crucial about the word *wrongs* in Step 5, because deep inside (unless we have thoroughly worked it through) we most likely feel there are many things "wrong" with ourselves — things that we use a lot of energy to hide. (Again, you might want to review Chapter 4.) Sometimes we take responsibility for things that were done to us at an early age; they weren't our fault, but we took the blame and the shame and were left with the guilt. Whatever the wrong is, it is not as serious as it seems. In fact, when you put it into a different, lighter perspective the label "wrong" may dissolve.

We need to deal with the concept of wrong or bad and the guilt that it brings. I knew a woman once who had killed two children in a car accident. It was clearly an accident; she was not at fault, but she blamed herself deep inside for this horrible event. Years later, she had two children, and I used to see them playing in the street unattended at very young ages. Their mother didn't feel she deserved the joy of motherhood because something deep inside told her she had taken it from someone else. It is important to note that she was unconscious of this process. She didn't consciously say to herself, "Well, I'll let my children risk getting killed by a car because I don't deserve them." And that is the point of my using this very disturbing example. This woman hadn't worked out her wrongs, and her guilt was punishing her; in turn, her family was also at risk. The main moral to the story and for this step is that it helps to confess our "wrongs" and work them out. That is the beauty of Twelve-Step programs. In an environment of unconditional acceptance, you can confess your wrongs, the things you keep punishing yourself for, and you will begin to view them in a different light. Just by admitting your wrongs in the presence of witnesses, you begin to remove the charge of guilt and shame that surrounds them. Listening to others' confessions is also healing.

Practice 5: The Angels and Step 5

If you are having difficulty admitting the exact nature of wrongs to yourself and to God, and in turn to another human being, start by admitting them to your angel sponsor — your guardian angel. You can do this in several ways. You can write a letter to your guardian, and really let yourself go with it. Or you can visualize a meeting of confession with your guardian angel, and visualize your guardian lovingly and unconditionally listening to your every word and thought. After you have practiced with your guardian angel, you need to find another human to talk with — someone you can trust. Ask the angels to guide you to this person if you don't have someone in your life you feel you can trust. Keep in mind that admission to another human being is essential to the success of this step; the angels are only for practice and guidance. We are cleansed by talking about our "wrongs" with someone we can trust.

An important element in this step is that of the "exact nature of our wrongs." Sometimes we think we have done something wrong, but we don't examine the exact nature of what it really is. So ask your angel guardian and sponsor for insight into the exact nature of your wrongs and of your rights. This will allow you greater understanding in how to progress beyond the wrongs. You may want to use a piece of paper and write the wrongs down and then connect them to the exact nature of how they manifest in your life. It helps to remember your angel cheerleaders. They love you no matter what you have done, and they are always there cheering you on to your higher self. Also remember that at this very moment you are a different person than the day and time of the wrongs you may have committed. That is why it is destructive to label people good and bad; these are just temporary ideas, but the labels have lasting negative outcomes. You are ever changing and your true inner nature is heading toward the light. So go with the angels; they are willing to carry you when needed. Let go of your past.

The essence of Step 5 is that confession is good for the soul.

A.A. *Step 6*

We were entirely ready to have God remove all these defects of character.

God did not make any human beings perfect, and I would hate to think of how boring the world would be if God had. Our imperfections make us great—when we are willing to transform them into our assets. What I mean by this is that our weakest areas deserve the most attention. So when we study ways of transforming ourselves in the positive direction, we can become effective teachers for others who are dealing with similar imperfections or weaknesses. Step 6 entails being willing to give up any thought of trying to be perfect; it entails letting go and letting God remove our defects rather than trying to rip them out ourselves. It also means being willing to be happy, and to create a positive life for ourselves. I find myself holding on to imperfections because if I let them go completely I would have to deal with being a very happy person who has fun most of the time. It is scary to let go of all of our defects; they are like security blankets. Willingness to be happy takes courage.

Practice 6: The Angels and Step 6

Being entirely ready to have God remove all your defects takes a lot of courage and trust. Think of a defect as a block that is

keeping you from being successful and happy. It could be something like low self-esteem. One thing to remember — and the angels will help you remember — is that change is best done slowly
and surely. Sudden changes in character are not the goal of this
step. Basically, saying you are *entirely* ready to have God remove
your defects means you will allow God's timing to prevail. Think
of some blocks you want to get rid of; bad habits, outmoded
beliefs, negative attitudes, and pain are all blocks. Make a list
and declare that you are letting the angels fly them away, take
them to God, and transmute them for the highest good of all
concerned. Visualize them leaving your being all in good time
and ask the angels for courage to let go of them. Trust in the
angels; everything will be okay!

The essence of Step 6 is to unblock the path to spiritual awareness and love.

A.A. *Step 7*

We humbly asked God to remove our shortcomings.

A lot of people I know who have been helped the most from
Twelve-Step programs had a negative attitude toward the programs in the beginning. They felt they were somehow too unique
and intelligent to be helped by such a program. In other words,
they were the opposite of humble in the beginning. We are all
unique, but we are also all connected. It helps to accept that
our humanity involves defects of character, even in the most
"evolved" of us. Humans have a tendency to compare themselves
to others and to compare others to others. When we compare,
we are looking to make a judgment of "better or worse than."
I don't like it at all when people compare me to someone else,
especially when it is a "better than" comparison. I don't want
to be better than, and I don't want to be the same as; I want to
be respected for my own experience of life and level of spiritual

and personal growth. In this area, we are all unique. We all have our own individual experience of life, and it stands on its own. Our greatest gift to others is to have total respect for their unique experiences of life. This will relieve most of our own shortcomings and bring us humility.

Practice 7: The Angels and Step 7

Meditate on the word *humble.* Think about humility as an attitude of innocence. Innocence means being free of self-analysis, free of comparisons. Each experience is new and beautiful. Connect with feelings of being naïve and free of judgments. Being humble is not an act of lowering yourself; it is an act of freeing yourself to be yourself and allowing others to be themselves. It is about ignoring the intellect that tells us we are superior. Humility is the love of being human. Ask the angels to help you restore balance in your life. Ask the angels to join you in your meditation on the concept of humility and to bring you a combination of wisdom and innocence, which will bring you serenity and peace.

The essence of Step 7 is that humility allows us to be whole beings.

A.A. Step 8

We made a list of all persons we had harmed, and became willing to make amends to them all.

People who are traveling a spiritual path sooner or later realize ways they might have been in the past that may have hurt someone. And they start to see how they have been hurt by others and may be holding on negatively to the past. This step tells us, once and for all, to come to a point where we can forgive the past and detach from it — to a point of forgiving others and forgiving ourselves. This step concerns unfinished business. If you are thinking you have harmed someone, that connection exists at a negative level for you. It casts a negative pall on your present life in some way. The key word here is *willing*. You may not yet know how to make amends, but you are cultivating the willingness to forgive yourself and come to a positive space in your mind with people from the past. With the angels on your side, you are also cultivating inside protection for making amends.

Practice 8: The Angels and Step 8

Have you ever really thought about the word *blame?* Blame means responsibility for a fault and criticism for doing a wrong. Self-blame and guilt are heavy weights we surround ourselves with when we can't change the past and it haunts us. If you blame yourself for something that happened in your past, start to allow a willingness to forgive and forget to emerge in your life. Holding onto the past can keep us from moving forward on the path to a happy and spiritual life. The past is only kept alive in our minds, and we may not even be keeping an accurate record of it. Get a piece of paper, call in your angels and make a list of all your unfinished business. The angels will want you to begin changing your perceptions of the past to a lighter tone, so start to think about humor. Some of these past memories may seem like they aren't very funny at all, but I can assure you they can take on a lighter weight in your life. Humor heals, and the angels use it often. So, after you make a list of people you have unfinished business with, because of your or their stubbornness, look for humor. The angels will help you. I guarantee that if it is a serious situation, one connected with false pride, humor is there somewhere. If you can't find the humor, look for the growth. When something painful happens to us, it can be the greatest accelerator of growth possible. At this point, after you have made your list, the main idea the angels want you to cultivate is being willing to lighten up and get ready to release the past by changing your perceptions of it.

The essence of Step 8 is the willingness to take yourself lightly by releasing hurts and wrongs from the past.

A.A. *Step 9*

We made direct amends to such people wherever possible, except when to do so would injure them or others.

This is basically the action to take to follow up on Step 8. One of the best feelings you can experience comes when you clear the air with someone you hurt or who hurt you. The act of forgiving is so simple but can be so blocked by false pride, stubbornness, and anger — so, although it is a simple act, it can be difficult to carry out. The important thing, once again, is to not get too serious and caught up with fear, anger, and hurt. If you are on a spiritual path and have followed the steps up to this one, you have gained great inner wisdom. You may not even know you have it, but it is alive within you in the form of spiritual strength. It is now time to call on the wisdom, humility, self-love, willingness, hope, and love you have gained and use these qualities to help you heal your past.

Practice 9: The Angels and Step 9

The essence of Step 9 is to make amends. Before physically making amends, you may want to do some energy work with the angels. All people have their own guardian angels. We can send our angels before us. If we are planning to meet with someone to make amends, we can ask for insight into the nature of our connection with them through our guardian angel. We can ask that our guardian angel meet with the other person's guardian angel and begin to heal the relationship. In fact, if making direct amends to certain people would hurt them, do it through the angels. (But, please, ask for insight to be sure you are not using angels as an excuse for avoiding making amends in person.) Also, if certain people are no longer in physical form, and you want forgiveness or closure with them, the angels are able to relay the message. One effective way to employ angel help is to write a letter to a person's guardian angel. Simply address it "To the highest angel of" or "To the guardian angel of." Then write and ask that a higher understanding of the situation come about. The results may not seem obvious in some cases — because we all have free will and individuals don't have to allow angel intervention. Cultivate knowing that in some way you have lightened the situation by bringing in the angels, because it is already done.

The essence of Step 9 is taking action to transform the past.

A.A. Step 10

We continued to take personal inventory and when we were wrong promptly admitted it.

This step represents a commitment to stay awake, to remain aware of what we do each day and how we affect others. Steps 8 and 9 cleaned up the past; now it is up to us to keep the present clean by forgiving ourselves and others at the appropriate time. If we are "wrong" in a situation, so what? Don't be attached; admit it and dissolve the label. If you haven't been successful with eliminating the issue of guilt, this step won't be of value to you. Guilt is self-focused punishment and clouds one's view of the present. It is selfish because it keeps the wrongs of the past alive, so that others cannot forgive us and go on. Guilt tells others, "Look I am punishing myself harshly. I know I hurt you, but I don't have to deal with that because look at the pain I have." So if you have any guilt left over from the previous steps, ask the angels to help you resolve it.

Practice 10: *The Angels and Step 10*

This step says: No more black-and-white thinking; think only in angel colors. There is so much color to the world. No two experiences are the same, and yet we are always grouping things together and comparing them to each other. Practicing black-and-white thinking is a defensive mechanism people adopt so they can feel certainty and assign reasons to events. This thinking can be taken even further to speaking in terms of good or bad people. If people decide they are good, then of course bad things are always happening around them and no one understands how good they are. If people view themselves as bad, then who cares what happens anyway—the whole world is bad. To think in the colors of the angels, we have to get rid of the notions of good and bad. Everything exists as a separate and distinct event, encompassing many aspects. The angels remind us there is always a way to view events with a positive attitude instead of a personal interpretation of doom and gloom. For this step, ask the angels to help you accept the present as it is—full of colors. And ask them to help you accept who you are and keep your mind light and positive. This helps you stay awake and aware, so your colorful actions originate from a space of love.

The essence of Step 10 is that you are alive; stay awake and aware, trust the colors of the angels, and don't engage in black-and-white thinking.

A.A. *Step 11*

We sought through prayer and meditation to improve our conscious contact with God as we understood God, praying only for knowledge of God's will for us and the power to carry that out.

This step can be summed up as: Thy will (not mine) be done. If we release ourselves from all of our earthly attachments and pray for God's will to be done in our lives, true magic takes place. This doesn't mean that we become nuns and monks; it means we begin to integrate the spiritual into our everyday life. The angels bring the kingdom of God to earth to help us recognize that we are spiritual beings having a human experience. We are here on the earth for a reason; otherwise we wouldn't be here. To make the most of our stay here, and to become bright lights that shine hope, we must open fully to the will of God. This is about surrendering our will to God, which in turn gives us incredible strength and power to conquer the trials of everyday life. We surrender and understand God through quiet meditation (listening to God) and by prayer (talking with God).

Practice 11: The Angels and Step 11

It is up to us to know that God is loving and unconditional. God does not punish us; we punish ourselves by not allowing the river to flow on its own. Regardless of your understanding of God, for the sake of this practice begin to get in touch with the loving abundance, the hope, and the protection God has for us through the angels. When you come to a space where you know God as unconditional love, it is easier to surrender and let go of our struggles with life. The angels guard your life force if you let them. Learn to trust and let go and you will live a happy life, full of joyfull moments. Meditate on the love and pray for guidance.

The essence of Step 11 is bringing the light of heaven to earth.

A.A. Step 12

Having had a spiritual awakening as the result of these steps, we tried to carry this message to alcoholics, and to practice these principles in all our affairs.

A spiritual awakening brings us to the realization that we can help others. We realize that helping others doesn't mean rescuing them, but loving them for who they are and where they are. We are now the light, and we transmit a message of hope to others automatically. This step works both ways; by taking our message of hope out to others, we help others and we help keep the message alive and well in ourselves. Our inner strength (God) is now what keeps us going, as opposed to the strength we thought we could get from others. By going out among others, we don't have the time for self-preoccupation with our little problems. We can take a step outside ourself and begin to really connect with others because our spiritual strength has centered us to know who we are. Therefore, we can offer our service to the universe.

Practice 12: The Angels and Step 12

It is time to do an angel step meeting, also known as an angel conference. It helps to get a piece of paper and draw a diagram of your meeting. You will need to use your imagination for this practice. Write "God and angels are here" somewhere on your paper. Bring in your personal angels (guardian angel/sponsor, muse, spirit guide, and so on) and start the conference. Think of areas in your life that need to be managed in a more positive way and assign an angel to help with each area. Go through the steps and assign angels to help you with any step you need support with. List some goals you want to achieve and assign an angel to each goal. List any bad habits or negative brain programs you may have and declare that they will change to the positive. Assign an angel to set up a signal in your brain each time the urge to be negative starts to take hold, so you can consciously change directions.

Think of people you know who need extra help. Write their names on the conference sheet and ask that special angel blessings go their way. If you want protection from certain people in your life, write their names and then draw a barrier of white light around them and declare that the angels are protecting you and transmuting the energy to the positive. Use the conference as a gauge to see where you are at the moment. You may want to do an ANGEL® card reading for extra insight (see Chapter 19 to find out where to get them). Do an angel conference whenever you want to clarify where you are at the moment and where you are heading. It is okay to change, so when you look back on the conference and you see a big change in your life, keep your attitude positive. Remember, the world steps back to let those who know where they are going pass by.

The essence of Step 12 is to keep ourselves clear and on track, so we can truly be of service.

Chapter 9

Personal Power

People habitually use only a small part of the powers which they possess and which they might use under appropriate circumstances.

William James

All of us here on earth have our own sources of personal power. Some people give their power away and end up feeling and thinking like victims; some go to the other extreme with their power and create situations that victimize others. Our power is energy we use to establish who we are. Life entails such a fine balance. If too much power was taken away from us while we were growing up, we may feel out of control and powerless, and this may cause us to look for power outside ourselves. If we were given too much power as children, we may have to overcome the "center of the universe syndrome" or a tendency toward vanity or narcissism. Either way, personal power depends on a delicate balance.

When we are centered, we have brought our personal power and life force totally within ourselves; we can control the flame.

If we are uncentered, the flame may rage out of control or be so dim someone may blow it out accidentally. The concept of power and balance is not a new one. What might be new for you is the idea that angels can help us keep our power in balance, and fight for us when we feel like victims. We may not see this fight or even know it is happening, but if we trust the angels they will always be there, cheering us on to victory. And, if we are going in the direction of too much power, they will offer gentle lessons designed to temper our flame.

At times we may rely on other people in our lives to define who we are and to give us an illusion of security. Doing this can cause problems. The only true security on this planet comes from within ourselves. Security is only an illusion; a true sense of security only exists at those times when we are happy with who we are. I'm not talking here about external happiness; I'm talking about knowing in your heart that wherever you are and whatever happens around you, it will be okay because you are basically happy and have resources for entertaining yourself. This is a truly magic power, one the angels love to play with. When you reach this magic way of being, the laws (and the angels) of the universe work in your favor and provide you with wonderful friends and interesting relationships. In contrast, if you are constantly looking for new friends and relationships with the belief that they will fill what is missing in your life, then people will be repelled. Again, this comes back around to being yourself— to being you, and only you. You are special, unusual, remarkable, and very capable of having what you want. When you know that truth deep inside yourself, others of like mind will know it, too, and be attracted to you. Then other people become embellishments to your life instead of disappointments.

Whoever you are right now, and whatever background you come from, you have your own personal power and if used in balance and harmony it will lead you to a happy and free state of being. You can change directions, reverse negative habits, break old molds, enjoy yourself, be someone new, start a new career, become an artist or a poet or whatever your heart desires — all it takes is energy put toward that particular goal. This energy comes from your own internal power source — your higher self, which the angels are in close contact with.

The practices in this chapter are designed to show you how angels can help you keep your personal power fresh and energized rather than stale or overwhelming, keep your personal power protected from negative influences, and learn to set appropriate boundaries.

Practice 1: Your Inner Wise Angel Guide

If we truly believe we are creating new consciousness, then we have to let go of old and crusty ways of being. Learning to adapt to and to relish change is an important practice. The practice of listening to our intuition automatically allows us to flow with change. Intuition is wisdom. Wisdom is balance and sound judgment. I am not talking about the judgment of right versus wrong, or good versus bad, but the judgment of what feels appropriate, what makes for a comfortable decision. Such judgments are personal to us and involve knowing ourselves well. We can learn a lot about ourselves through our intuition.

Angels can help us understand what intuition means in a personal way. Angels are actually in charge of a large part of our intuitive self. Viewing intuition from the perspective of angel consciousness, we can say that intuition is our way of tapping into a higher power for guidance and awareness. You may have heard the saying that "God works in mysterious ways." We say this because sometimes our rational mind cannot make sense out of the intuitive side of life. You may be more familiar with your rational mind than you are with your intuitive mind. Our rational mind needs logical explanations, analysis, definitions, reasons, and cautions. Our intuitive nature is spontaneous and difficult to define; therefore, it is better not to define it! Learning to listen to our intuition takes practice. Establishing a habit of listening to our inner wisdom brings us closer to our completed self.

First, let me clarify what I believe our higher self to be. I'm not using the word *higher* as a judgment, as if the higher self is good, our middle self is just so-so, and our lower self is bad. The point isn't whether these selves are good or bad, because that doesn't capture their real essence. When we feel complete, all of our selves are integrated and acting in the same direction. The higher self represents wisdom, our connection with the angelic realm, and our connection with the higher power in our life. The higher self is also our intuitive nature, the source of the unique and creative way we have of giving love to the world. The middle self is generally the part of ourselves we know well, and we use it to relate to the uncertain aspects of life in a comfortable way. Our middle self reacts to the everyday aspects of our lives in a way that isn't too heavy or too light. The lower self could be thought of as an amalgam of the parts of ourselves that we aren't so familiar with. I use the word *lower* in this case to represent the act of repressing—pushing these qualities downward, burying them so that we don't have to deal with them all the time. Constantly dealing with them would get too intense and heavy—so it's great to have a storage space for these aspects to wait until the higher self pulls them out and deals with them from the perspective of wisdom and light. The ideal state is when we are integrated, whole beings. To get to this point, we need to do a lot of work/play, but one good starting place is listening to our intuition as a way to know our own special path and the qualities we have brought into this life.

Listening to our intuition is the same as listening to our angels. The messages may reach us in ways we aren't used to, such as noticing bizarre and interesting thoughts or phrases taken out of context, or receiving odd phone calls or unexpected meetings; I don't want to limit your ideas about this, because your intuition is personal to you, just as your own experience of angels is.

For this practice, go into angel alpha state and begin to imagine your wise inner angel guide. You can think of this guide as either a separate being from your higher self, as your higher self, or simply as part of your inner nature. Do what feels most comfortable; try to get past the need to define. As you go deeper into angel alpha, begin to feel at one with the light, a oneness with all creation in this timeless place where you are free from the heaviness of the earth and your body. Imagine you are meeting your wise angel guide. Is your wise angel guide sitting in a large comfortable chair or lying back on a colorful bed of clouds? What does this angel look like?

Ask your wise angel guide to give you a clear example of your own intuition. It may seem that a small clear voice speaks to you. (Again, remember that listening to your angelic wisdom will never cause you fear or anxiety; stop if you begin to have negative images or feelings.) Intuition may take the form of an image or gut feeling. Just relax; if it seems as if nothing is happening, this is important, too. We are so accustomed to things happening that when nothing happens we think something is wrong, but it is just fine. Have fun with your wise angel guide; this space you are in is the source of divine humor and bliss. It is also a place to reunite with your inner child, so develop a sense of wonder and playfulness when you are with your wise angel guide.

If you have made a strong connection, use this moment to ask for insight into your present state of affairs. If you know of a brain program you want to edit, do so now. Have fun for a while and use this time "wisely." When you come out of angel alpha state, thank the angels for bringing you closer to a completed, whole state of being and ask them to keep the momentum going.

Another fun way to get in touch with your wise inner angel is to use ANGEL® cards. (See Chapter 19 to find out where to get them.) Take a deck of ANGEL® cards, shuffle them, and then imagine your wise angel. Think the words "My wise angel says," then pick a card to represent what your wise angel has to say to you at that moment. Pick two, three, or however many cards you desire. Use your imagination and you will discover other uses for the cards.

Practice 2: Boundaries and Balance

Babies need several things to keep them alive; chief among these is love. I mean this literally. It is a known fact that even when babies get enough food to eat, if they are not touched, loved, and held they will cease to exist. Babies and small children are "needy"; they depend on the kindness of adults for their existence. If they are not taken care of properly, their survival program may begin to take the form of "Someone please save me." If only someone nice and wonderful would come and take me away and give me love and ice cream all day, life would be great! Some people who were not properly taken care of when they were very young are still looking for this someone to save them. Sometimes it even seems as if they have found someone, but then the someone lets them down and they are sure someone else will be by to pick them up and wash the pain away. What is wrong with this picture? What is missing?

One main piece missing from this picture is trust and independence. Can we ever really trust anyone except ourselves? Is it fair to expect to trust someone under our own conditions? It seems unreasonable and extremely conditional. For the "trust someone else" scenario to work, the "trustworthy" people have to follow all the rules we have set up, which makes us think they are trustworthy. On the other hand, if we trust in ourselves we will not need to "trust" others, and both parties will be free to be who they truly are. Trusting others won't become an issue; if fact, we won't even need the idea in our belief system. This may sound a bit confusing since the idea of trusting others is such a nice one. I am getting back to the first concept in this chapter, the one of personal power and victimhood. As an occasional representative of the angels, I have the distinct impression that they want all of us to feel powerful and never like victims. One reason angels exist is so we can have a force to trust in. Trusting the angels will help keep us from feeling at the mercy of uncaring people or conditions.

Once again, the issue of balance is essential. We must have balance and a center to our being. Any feeling of neediness that pulls us in the direction of someone other than ourselves pulls us away from our center. Developing boundaries is a good way to establish our center. When a feeling of neediness becomes strong in your mind, establish a boundary that it can't cross. Decide and declare that this need has to stay inside the boundary of you to be fulfilled. It cannot go out in the world and look for someone or some situation to remedy it. You may not immediately think you have the resources to fulfill the need inside your own boundaries, but you do; just be patient and ask your angels. Do not try to second-guess the angels with a belief that the situation is impossible.

Draw a picture of yourself; it doesn't have to be elaborate—a stick figure is fine. Now draw your boundary—a large circle around the figure of yourself. Inside the boundary, write in things that you have let go past the boundary, things that have caused you problems. Think of needs you are sure you have—these can be anything; each person's boundary will contain different contents. You might note a need for love, security, or happiness. After you have written down these needs, examine them with the notion that only you can really take care of these needs from within. Now write down your inner resources. Draw pictures of angels surrounding each need, or just write angels around it and declare that you and the angels will take care of all your needs. Surround each need with a positive thought of success. Check it every once in a while and update it. You can think of it as your happiness center chart.

At this point in your life, you are all you need. I don't mean to say that other people do not matter in your life; they certainly do! It is just much more fun to think of other people as an embellishment to your life instead of a necessity — other people to share interesting moments with, and to bring one another's creative side into view. Being centered is of the utmost importance these days. Find your center, and ask the angels to help you protect it. This way you will have your own personal power and no one can make you a victim.

Practice 3: Low Batteries Lead to Negative Openings

Sometimes we get so run down that we feel as if we are being psychically attacked from unknown sources. Whether an attack is actually being waged doesn't matter; the feelings are real. Think about your body as running on a rechargeable battery. When the battery is low, your light is dim, and your thoughts are not clear and bright. When your battery is recharged by taking care of yourself properly, you will shine brightly and get a clear reading on situations in your life.

Many things can make our batteries run low. It is no secret that dealing with life's ups and downs is an exhausting process. That is why we need sleep, movement, and nourishing food to keep ourselves in good shape. Think about a time when you were very active, running around crazily and off your center. It may have been an exciting time, but what happened when all the frenetic activity stopped? Did you feel depleted and depressed? A lot of people do. A lot of people spend much of their life off center, depleting their energy supply with too much stimulation, then sinking low — stressed out and unable to cope. Then, after a time of depression, they are up and running again.

I am not judging this type of life-style as right or wrong, but I want to point out a few things people who live this way have shared with me, and that I have learned from my own experiences. The low periods can be very frightening times when people with a frenetic life-style feel they have lost their power to cope. This can lead normally positive people to begin thinking negatively about many things — about themselves, other people, and their lives. Everything takes on a negative and pessimistic color. They become hard on themselves and claim there must be something wrong with their personality. Sometimes they imagine demons are after them who want them to fail and be unhappy. Again, I'm not judging whether or not these perceptions are facts; that doesn't matter. I want you to know that you can prevent this depletion from taking over and that the angels can help you in many ways.

There are many ways we run our batteries dangerously low. For one, any type of chemical substance, including alcohol and other drugs, can wear down our psychic energy. So can working at a job we hate. Harboring feelings of resentment or hatred toward a person or place, and feeling as if we don't have the power to resolve these feelings, wears down our energy. So does being in an unhappy relationship. Using our energy to rescue or control others (which always causes more work in the long run) also depletes us. I'm sure you can think of many other examples.

These are just a few examples of temporary situations that may give us the feeling of being powerless. These times can be positive turning points when we open our minds and let the angels in to rework a few attitudes and change a few situations. Take time-outs during the day to check in with your angels — your inner nature. Visualize a quick recharging session with your angels. Do this in whatever way works for you. One way could be stopping activity and sitting down with a tall, cool glass of pure water. As you sip the water, imagine the water as pure, clean energy. It will reach your center, your battery, and reenergize you. Nature works best in a state of balance. And your body is a part of nature's balance, so make sure you take care of it. Protect your center and your sensitivity. Keep out the unwanted negatives, and don't forget the angels make a great barrier to these unwanted forces.

Chapter 10

Angelic Understanding of Human Relationships

Our relationships with other people can teach us powerful lessons about ourselves. Human relationships usually evolve into forms such as friendship, marriage, a love affair, an acquaintance, or a family tie. The form usually has certain rules for behavior on our part and that of the other person. Of course, both players are unique beings, so even though the form and basis seem the same in our minds, the chemistry is unique. Because the world is changing so quickly these days, our relationship forms need to be able to change quickly, too. Trouble and emotional pain may come when won't accept progressive changes in the forms our relationships take. For example, if our relationships are the basis of our happiness, when they change forms we risk losing our happiness. If we base our happiness on ourselves and get rid of the conditions and labels we put on our relationships, then we will be free to experience the wonders of other human beings.

When the angels come to play in your life, you never know who they will bring your way or who will get out of your way.

The important issue is trust: Trust in yourself and trust in the angels; then you can follow your own path. The people you meet on your path are like mirrors for you. The main reason I am including this chapter is because as you grow, expand your mind, and break old patterns and molds, you will encounter people in your life who are not at the same stage as you. At times, this can cause problems and may even cause fear. You may think to yourself, How could I get along without this person in my life? If you trust yourself and the angels, everything will work out fine. The lessons will be powerful, but they will bring you closer to knowing who you really are, and who you can honestly be for someone else.

We live at an amazing time; sometimes it may feel as if there were water rising around us. But there are no human lifeguards available to save those who will not let go of their old ways and who are drowning in the rising water. When we try to save someone else, our efforts backfire. The time is coming when there will be no more victims and rescuers. We all must save ourselves; luckily for us, there are "spiritual lifeguards"—the angels! If you are drowning, ask the spiritual lifeguards to save you; they are always there. Trust and let go. If you do drown, you will be spiritually reborn.

Old excuses for not "getting it together" and old ways of manipulating the world around you won't work if you are on a spiritual path. You may be noticing the changes in your life and in the lives of people around you. If not, you will soon. Those of us who feel strong and spiritually awakened must become subtle teachers for those who are struggling.

The distinction between rescuer and friend must consistently be respected. A friend listens and offers insight when asked; a rescuer offers help and shortcuts without being asked. I am not saying that helping others is always rescuing; if a friend needs money, asks for a loan, agrees to pay it back, and you give it to him or her, this is not necessarily rescuing. However, we must examine our own motives and thoughts, staying spiritually awake so we are acting from a higher aspect of ourselves. Remember, rescuers help without being asked, and then interfere, project, and try to control.

When those you love are drowning, you may feel much grief and guilt, especially if you are too attached to stand back and let them hit the bottom. However, letting them hit bottom may be the most positive thing that will ever happen to both of you. This is where the spiritual lifeguards come in again. If you feel powerless because people close to you are going through a difficult time, a spiritual emergency, ask their personal lifeguards — their guardian angels — to help them save themselves. Contact the angels around them and send them love light to heal their center. This is not a time to try to make it easier by rescuing them.

The practices in this chapter are meant to help you understand your relationships by accessing your angels for higher insight and wisdom. First, I discuss meetings between guardian angels, a very useful practice in these times of "rising water."

Practice 1: Meetings Between Guardian Angels

Consider the closest thing to an angel on earth – your mind or soul. In the blink of an eye, your mind – which is spirit like an angel – can go from the room you were married in to the edge of the universe.

Being spirits, angels move like our imaginations – instantly, as near or far as they want, to the past, present or future.

John Ronner

Guardian angels can be very effective communication assistants in our personal relationships. Our angels can give us insight into our feelings and into the soul intensity level and lessons of our relationships with others. Some connections we have with others are inexplicably strong. Whatever the connection, there is always a higher meaning for our being with someone. We all have guardian angels, and our guardian angels can help reveal the higher aspects of our relationships. We might as well take advantage of our guardians' ability to help with our relationships; human relationships are very important.

Accessing this special angel contribution to our relationships is very simple. Basically, all we have to do is ask our guardian angel to meet with the other person's guardian. If there is something that you are finding difficult to communicate to the other person verbally, tell your angel to tell the other person's angel for you. Then know that the two angels are meeting on the behalf of both parties and working things out. Use this technique however you see fit, whenever you feel the need. Sometimes it helps to write a letter to the other person's guardian angel. After you bring the angels in, look for signs of their influence. Pay attention to messages you receive that help you understand what is happening on a deeper level.

Go into angel alpha state and let your imagination run freely, then fantasize about why certain people are present in your life, asking the angels for insight into the depth and importance of these relationships. Follow a stream of consciousness — when a name or face appears in your mind, follow the stream wherever it may lead. Go on a tour of your relationships. Ask yourself what your role has been with specific people. What form has the relationship taken, and will the form be able to support the relationship in coming times? Visualize meetings between your guardian and the guardians of others in your life, and ask for messages, insights, and ways to communicate more fully by removing emotional blocks and misunderstandings.

You may want to write about the experience to understand more clearly what it all means. Writing allows you to save it until it makes sense at a later date. When you bring angels in your life to help communicate with others, I want to remind you that the angels respect the free will of all concerned. In other words, there is no way to manipulate or influence other people with angels. The most valuable thing the angels can offer you when you involve them in your relationships is understanding. When a thought of someone comes into your mind, send out a beam of angel light to that person and your connection will lighten and expand in some way. The less action you yourself take, the better. It will all work out for the highest good of all concerned.

Communication between family members can be enhanced by acknowledging the family angel for peace, and communicating love within the family. Discover family guardian angels and how to use them for effective communication and understanding. Family forms are being challenged and changed these days. Family guardians provide valuable help in adjusting to possible changes or struggles within the family form.

Practice 2: Synergistic Friendship and Relationships

The meeting of two personalities is like the contact of two chemical substances: if there is any reaction, both are transformed.

C. G. Jung

Synergistic means that the combined effects of two things exceeds the sum of their individual effects. Synergistic friendship means that the combined effects of two minds goes beyond what you could imagine doing alone. My friend John Harricharan uses this term, and it describes our friendship well. It seems that each time I talk to him, thoughts and ideas are generated that go way beyond our individual minds. I have other synergistic relationships, and they exist on a very high plane of awareness and respect.

Soul mates have synergistic effects on each other also. When two people meet in a soul-mate relationship, old ideas and beliefs crumble and new ideas and insight are created. In other words, a transformation takes place. With some people, this transformation signifies the start of one's life work really taking off.

Partnerships that are synergistic are great for generating new ideas and projects that have a high potential for success. When you recognize angels in a synergistic relationship, you will travel amazing avenues. Think about your friendships, partnerships, and relationships, and look for synergy. If you need some extra synergistic energy in your relationships, bring in the angels. If the relationship is the opposite of synergy, think about peacefully breaking free from it. If you find it is time to make such a break, the angels will help you with the right timing, so that everything works out for the highest good of all.

Practice 3: Allowing the Winds of Heaven to Dance Between You

Instead of impulsively making a move from your side, you allow a move from the other side, which is learning to dance with the situation. You do not have to create the whole situation; you just watch it, work with it and learn to dance with it. So then it does not become your creation, but rather a mutual dance.

Chogyam Trungpa, in Challenge of the Heart

One way to keep an angelic influence in relationships is to allow room for the winds of heaven to flow between you. Within the winds of heaven are the angels. You must leave space for the angels to play. If you have ever gotten too close to someone, you may know what it is like when the angels don't have the room to play between you. Things get stale, dull, and lifeless. When the winds of heaven dance between you, then each party is creating the relationship equally. And the angels are there encouraging fun and happy times.

Think about some of your close relationships and ask yourself if the angels have enough room to dance in the winds of heaven between you. Visualize them dancing, playing, and celebrating life. That is what friendship is all about. Next time you are with

a close friend, visualize the angels around both of you and welcome any chance to laugh and giggle. This will get the angels
going, and who knows what silly things will happen.

And, always remember, if a friend is having a difficult time
and you are there to help, declare that winds of heaven inspire
you to stay centered in yourself and inspire your friend to find
her or his center also. The interesting thing about leaving space
between you and someone else is that it makes for a stronger
bond, based on respect. That type of bond stays strong regardless of the miles or inches between you. Heavenly connections
are the best!

Part Four

Angelic Accelerators

About Part Four:

Sensing Angels

For us humans, the world of the angels is a world of the unseen; that is, we do not rely on eyesight to discover this world. We experience the angelic realm through feelings and intuition, our sixth sense. To see angels, we do not need our eyes; they are visible to us in our mind's eye, through our insight. To hear angels, we must listen to our inner thoughts, not to external sounds. To smell angels, we do not need our noses, for when they leave the scent of heavenly roses or jasmine it intoxicates our soul. To touch angels, we do not need our fingers; we must tune into our ethereal sense of touch and imagine what light feels like as it touches our energy system. To use our sense of taste to know angels, we must imagine something pure and sweet, with no aftertaste or trace of bitterness, like a cloud of cotton candy spun with the sugar of heavenly fruit.

When we combine all of our senses this way, we have an extra power of full perception, the sixth sense. The angels use certain facets of our sixth sense to help us accelerate our growth and potential for greatness. These accelerators depend on inner feelings; they are not just thoughts, and they are not concrete concepts we can play around with logically. They are the angels' tricks of the trade, available to us and designed to help us be our personal best. This section of the book delves into some of these angelic accelerators: hope, faith, grace, gratitude, and for-giveness. These accelerators are components of true happiness and love. Happiness and love are not commodities; we cannot buy or trade them, and they have nothing to do with logic or explanation. We can only train ourselves to be open and ready to accept love and happiness into our hearts, and we see the proof of love's existence through the large and small miracles that we create with the angels.

Chapter 11

Faith, Hope, and Optimism

Optimism is positive thinking lighted up. Some chronic objectors to anything that smacks of hopefulness have decried positive thinking as an overly bright view of life and a kind of jaunty disregard of pain and trouble in this world. Some people have distorted my emphasis, often deliberately, I have felt. Others simply have misunderstood.

The positive thinker is a hard-headed, tough-minded and factual realist. He sees all the difficulties, and I mean all, and what's more he sees them clearly . . . which is more than can be said for the average negative thinker. The latter invariably sees everything in shadowy discoloration. But the positive thinker, unlike the negativist, does not allow difficulties and problems to depress him, and certainly not to defeat him. He looks expectantly beyond all acknowledged difficulties for creative solutions. In other words, he sees more than difficulties – he tries to see the solutions of those difficulties.

Norman Vincent Peale, The Tough-Minded Optimist

Hope and Optimism

Optimism entails much more than just a good mood. True optimism takes strength and courage, and lots of it. It is not for the weak or the fearful. It is not easy to look honestly at the ridiculous, nonsensical state of the human condition and still see the light of possibilities and solutions. It is much easier to be a pessimist; there is so much support out there to maintain a constant state of negative thinking. Optimists are virtually swimming upstream, but it is worth it because the true opposite of optimism is not just pessimism — it is despair, doubt, and depression. Optimism refuses to accept despair and doubt. Optimism guides us in a natural and spontaneous fashion toward achieving our highest goals and maintaining our highest values.

We are faced with increasing polarities on this planet. Many people are seeking the higher power in their lives, and the world is alive with the dazzling light of truth, but at the same time the darkness has become increasingly dark. Light is powerful and the angels are with us all the way, cheering us on, providing daylight in our minds. We must not accept gloomy statistics; those who make it against all odds are not pessimists — they are optimists! Optimists may have to travel a bumpy road at times, but no one has to accept negative judgments and gloomy statistics provided by pessimists.

In *Messengers of Light,* I wrote a chapter on becoming an "optimystic." An optimystic is a person who combines the essence of a mystic with the hope and magic of an optimist. Hope is the main ingredient for becoming an optimystic. Hope is a feeling of trust and assumption that all will turn out well. There is no such thing as false hope. If you are hoping for something and some pessimists come along to nay say you, tell them to keep their negative thoughts to themselves. In my most extreme moments, I would like to have a law against negative statements given to positive people! Sometimes a negative statement can be worse than a punch in the face. We have the right to hope for and create a positive climate in our minds, which in turn will bring us positive outcomes, and this right should be protected. I also think we should be protected from doctors who enjoy playing God by telling patients with diseases how long they have to live.

Some may want to argue and say that hope means you are not living in the moment, and so there must be something wrong with hoping. Truly living in the moment at all times is something that takes place inside of us; it basically means staying awake and aware. Being awake and aware does not have to entail pain, and that is why hope exists. Show me a happy and positive person who deep inside does not value the essence of hope, and I will truly be surprised.

If we practiced giving hope to everyone we met, and everyone we met gave us hope, hope would reign and doomsday would never come. Since this utopia is not reality, we must create it in our imagination, and we can do this by bringing in faith. Hope and faith exist together synergistically.

Faith

For me, faith is another word for positive thinking. When real faith grips you, you develop a mind-set that looks for the best in everything, refuses to give up, finds a way around (or through) every obstacle, and presses on to victory.
                    Norman Vincent Peale, My Favorite Quotations

Hope and faith are gifts from God, or our higher power. For faith to work in our lives as an angelic accelerator, we must recognize the fact that it does not exist in a pure form unless we form a deep conviction in our hearts that God is a real presence in our lives — the main guiding light on our path. To have real faith, we must know a higher power in our lives, in our hearts, in our souls, and in our minds. The practice of faith strengthens our personal relationship with this higher power. So where do we meet God? Right here and now; the ground you stand on is holy ground.

When our reality is truly "faith in God, in God we trust," our fear cannot exist. If you truly have trust and faith in God, then you have no reason to fear anybody or anything in this life. Fear is a strong power, but faith is much stronger. An old saying goes, "Fear knocked at the door. Faith answered. No one was there." Another negative pattern that cannot operate in the presence of faith is excessive worry. Worry is torment; it creates doubts and anxieties to sustain itself, which in turn takes the worrier away from optimism, hope, and faith.

Faith is made up of angels. When you declare your faith, a path of angels is formed from your being up through the gates of heaven to God. Faith is an inner knowing that takes you beyond belief to a state of oneness with loving trust. Faith is positive energy focused on a desire or conviction that you want to come to pass. Faith is very powerful energy in its raw state. Faith becomes brighter through right action, and loses its glow with inertia. When you declare faith, to keep it working you must make it you — that is, you must become one with it so you are not thinking about it but only guided by it. Your actions and practices will bring about desired outcomes when you unite with your faith. Angels are always there to guard your positive thinking and faith; so when you lose some of your faith, ask for more from God and the angels.

Sometimes, having faith in a particular situation may not make sense to you. In other words, you may try to second-guess the angels by figuring that they couldn't possibly help you in a certain situation; you create doubt and cancel your faith. The angels are very clever when a human being needs help. In one of my favorite types of angel experiences, angels appear in human form to guard people even when they themselves don't see the angels, but other humans who may have bad intentions toward them do.

For example, two young African American men were riding their bikes down a secluded road in the South when a car full of four large, racist white men pulled up to them, knocked them off their bikes, and began to threaten them with brutality. The young man who told me this story said that at that time he asked God to please help them, but even as he asked he couldn't really figure out how—given the circumstances—any miraculous change could take place. A moment later, a car pulled up and a priest of very small stature got out of the car and started to walk toward the group. The four white men took one look at the priest, rushed to their car, jumped in, and sped off as if they had seen an army coming after them. The two African Americans were a bit confused, although relieved, and told the priest what the situation was. He chuckled and told them about the ways of angels. Apparently the four white men saw much more than one little priest get out of a car. Unfortunately, this story has to do with racism—something I don't like to remind you of, but it is a blight that is still too prevalent in our society.

I have read about and been told many angel stories like this, which range from stories of whole armies of angels appearing to scare off opposing forces to stories of one person intending to harm another at a vulnerable time and then admitting he or she was scared off by the two big men walking with the vulnerable person, even though the potential victim was walking alone. Have faith, because angels can distract or change the perception of others who may hurt us. Some friends of mine live on very special forest land; often when they leave it for periods of time, people have come to visit and can't find it. My friends have since discovered that the angels put a veil over it when they aren't home that confuses people's perception. So, even when your imagination cannot come up with a way in which the angels can help you, don't limit them; let them do their work and have faith—you are protected. And always remember to *ask* for help, no matter what the stage of your own faith.

It may be difficult (though not impossible) for a person who is too comfortable (not inclined to be in dangerous situations), to practice true faith. Those in "trouble" develop the deepest faith because it is necessary for survival. The irony here is that those in comfort need faith more, because they are more susceptible to depression and boredom and may feel spiritually unfulfilled until they have faith in themselves and get out there and practice their unique spirituality as a gift to the world.

Faith and hope are not tangible substances; they are not the same to everyone. Angelic accelerators such as faith and hope take different forms in each of our lives, because each of us is a unique facet of God's light. Being faithful means being conscientious, true, and accurate. We see the truth, however uncomfortable it is, and we have faith in ourselves to create a positive outcome and come up with creative solutions; this in turn gives us hope, making us true optimists (optimystics). Angels are manifestations of God's essences and energy forces, capable of transmitting accelerators such as faith and hope to us humans. They are gifts to accelerate our spiritual growth and bring us peace in our hearts. When we are happy and mentally at peace, we are one with God and the angels.

Practice 1: Creating a Personal Hope Meter

Prometheus was feeling sorry for humanity, so he went to Zeus, the supreme deity in Greek mythology, and asked his permission to allow humans to have fire. Zeus refused, saying that fire was only for the gods. So Prometheus stole fire and gave it to humans. Zeus was furious with Prometheus and angry with the humans for the way they used fire, and decided to punish both Prometheus and humanity. He created a beautiful and somewhat silly woman named Pandora and gave her insatiable curiosity. He also gave her a sealed jar and warned her not to open it. Hermes brought her to earth to marry Epimetheus and live among the mortals. Pandora soon became dissatisfied with life and allowed her insatiable curiosity to get the best of her, so she opened the jar. Zeus had filled the jar with greed, envy, vanity, slander, and various other ills and misfortunes to befall humanity. He put hope at the bottom of the jar, thinking all the other contents would kill it anyway — but Pandora closed the jar just in time for hope to remain.

Hope is a value; it is one of my most important values. When I ignore hope, I feel as if I'm in troubled waters, but when I nurture hope and create situations for it to thrive, life becomes smooth sailing. When I focus on all the ills and misfortunes let out of Pandora's jar, I temporarily lose hope for the future. These ills, such as greed and slander, corrupt almost every corner of our society. Greed puts men and women of God in jail, and the greed of big business is destroying Mother Earth. Greed haunts us wherever we turn, so it is up to us to keep hope alive in our hearts — and to create the future for the highest good of all concerned. It is not easy to keep hope alive, especially when you live with open eyes, but important goals are not always easy. One reason I work with children and young teenagers whenever I get the chance is because they give me hope. They are the future, and they continually amaze me. There is no such thing as teaching children; as far as I am concerned, they are the teachers.

To create a personal hope meter, keep a journal or notebook on hand. First, create a trust fund of hope, including situations and things that give you hope. Start thinking about hope, what it means to you, and what in your life encourages it. Please don't make a fund of what discourages it — your own Pandora's jar — because it is not worth the time. Let me remind you not to base too much of your hope on other people. In other words, do not hope for someone to come and rescue you; believe me, this is not what you want. Hope for the strength to trust the angels and yourself in any situation. Start your hope fund; you can deposit more later as your resources grow. To create your hope meter, draw a simple figure that represents a meter. On one end, write the word *hopeful,* and on the opposite end write the word *hopeless.* In the middle, write *neutral.* Check yourself out with the hope meter every day. When your hope is low, take out a withdrawal from your hope fund. An example might be a chapter in a book to read, going to the park and watching children play, seeing an inspiring movie, visiting a fun friend and discussing what gives your friend hope, or simply sitting quietly and asking the angels to please bring you some hope. Hope is a survival instinct, especially now.

Practice 2: Counting Your Blessings Instead of Sheep

Cultivating gratitude is extremely important. It is easy to go on day after day without giving thanks to God for the wonderful blessings God and the angels have brought your way. A good time to practice gratitude is right before you go to sleep. Relax and think about your life at the present, about what happened today, yesterday, or at any time that gave you hope, that made you happy, that changed your perception in a positive direction. Now think about what happened that made you uncomfortable, worried, fearful, and so on. These are also blessings because right now you are going to declare them so and thank God and the angels for the chance to be positive, hopeful, and creative in solving these challenging moments. Don't worry about the particulars at this time; just declare them blessings and give thanks — the pieces will fall into place later. When you have done this, thank God that more blessings are coming your way, and thank God for the faith you have deep in your heart that tells you all is well. The angels will hear this and sing an extra song in your honor, and they will always be with you to encourage the positive.

Practice 3: Worry Time-outs

Stopping worrying is not very easy, is it? But getting rid of excessive worry is always to your benefit when you are on a path toward creating unconditional happiness. When I simply ignore my worries, they don't go away, and when they get to be too much I know it is time to sit down and do some planning with the angels. The first thing you can do is set aside a time to worry each day if you need to. Give yourself some quiet time to get centered, get out your journal if you are keeping one, and, when you are ready, start worrying. Worry as much as you want; worry until it hurts! While you are worrying, start to list root words that come to your mind. Sometimes I draw a pressure cooker in the middle of a page, and write my root worries inside. Then I draw lines to other worries that are connected to the root worry.

For example, if money is a root worry, what things branch out from that main worry? After you have had a good worry fest, take note that the angel worry extinguishers have been alerted and are now with you to take care of the next step—solutions. If you are keeping track of worries in your drawing of a pressure cooker, add arrows to the outside to relieve pressure and write down some solutions—solutions are anything you can think of that would help the worry. If you're worried about something negative like a long drive in traffic, think of a way to use that time positively—listen to tapes or make a tape yourself, or talk to yourself. If you are feeling too much love and find it hard to handle, declare trust in yourself. Worries range from very intense to slightly serious, so handle them that way. If there are some that are just too much, turn them directly over to the angels. After you are through, declare that you would like help from heaven in following through with the solutions. Now comes the hard part: You can't worry for another twenty-four hours! When a worry pops up, make it leave quickly; you will get back to it later. Right now you are creatively being your best and most lighthearted self, and the angels are pleased.

Chapter 12

The Art of Moving Forward Gracefully

Amazing grace! How sweet the sound
That saved a wretch like me!
I once was lost, but now am found,
Was blind, but now I see.

'Twas grace that taught my heart to fear,
And grace my fears relieved;
How precious did that grace appear
The hour I first believed!

Through many dangers, toils and snares,
I have already come;
'Tis grace hath brought me safe thus far,
And grace will lead me home.

And when we've been there ten thousand years,
Bright shining as the sun,
We'll have no less days to sing God's praise
Than when we first begun.

John Newton

Grace is a gift from God, a moment of God's allowance and love. Grace offers a moment of pure radiant holiness, a moment of oneness with the full beauty and joy of heaven. We cannot pay for grace, nor earn it with our good works, piety, or human strength; the only thing we can do on our part is to be open to receiving it. Angels are the ministers of grace waiting behind the scenes to guide us to this divine state of being. Angels are ministers of grace because they engineer all the miracles, large and small, that go along with a state of grace — including serendipity, synchronicity, humor, decency, love, compassion, and mental peace.

Simply put, grace is a moment when we allow ourselves to be loved unconditionally by God. The moment may last for a split second or it can last for days or years; it all depends on how often we make ourselves available to grace. Grace can be a way of life, a way of letting God's love lead our way. If grace is God's love, and God's love is always available to us, why does the state of grace come and go? Sometimes we "edge God out" with our ego, and forget to ask for God's love and guidance. Also, we may be touched by grace every day of our lives and fail to recognize it or be aware of it.

When I was in college, I was excited to learn about the concept of invulnerable children. Invulnerable children are people who despite the most incredibly adverse situations during childhood, such as mental and physical abuse, dysfunctional and mentally ill people surrounding them, neglect, poverty, and so forth, grew up to become successful adults and exceptionally loving parents. I personally know several adults who were invulnerable children, and they are inspiring and loving people. When I hear stories of their childhoods, I can hardly believe what I'm hearing, but they made it through and used the events of their childhoods to further themselves and their creativity. A lot of people become "textbook cases," meaning they were treated badly when they were young and as adults fall into negative patterns easily explained by their childhoods. But no one, not the world's best psychiatrist, can give a simple answer concerning why some people make it despite all odds. M. Scott Peck says, in his book *The Road Less Traveled,* "All we can say is that there is a force, the mechanics of which we do not fully understand, that seems to operate routinely in most people to protect and to foster their mental (and physical) health even under the most adverse conditions." I am sure you know what I understand this force to be—God and the angels.

I am not telling anyone to believe in God or a higher power; human beings have free will. It is interesting to me, though, that when people truly hit rock bottom and pick themselves up, the one thing that most people say transformed them and brought them back was turning to a higher power (in their own fashion) and asking for guidance out of their pit.

Whoever you are and however you got where you are, whatever problems you have or don't have, whatever personality you have, whatever your childhood was like, there is a way to find the grace of God and the angels and to move gracefully forward on your own individual spiritual path. There is always a positive to every negative, and it is our gift of free will that gives us the choice to choose the positive.

It is not easy to define grace without talking about God or a higher power, but I'm not apologizing for talking about God. I'm also not promoting any particular religion or belief system, nor am I saying there is only one way to find a higher power in your life. Grace has nothing to do with how we are perceived by others, only with how good we feel from within and how willing we are to forgive ourselves for not living down to anyone else's negative expectations.

Practice 1: Morning Declaration

Wake up every morning and say, "I can hardly wait to see what God and the angels have in store for me today." When you say this, mean it; don't fear what God has in store for you, but be willing to accept fully what God has planned. This may take some discipline on your part, but you don't have to make it a big deal. Just grow into it; treat this philosophy like a new shoe — at first it is tight and uncomfortable, but soon it molds to your foot and fits comfortably and easily.

I can't really tell you how to have grace, because it is a gift from God, but if you follow certain practices and thought patterns, you put yourself in the right place and the right time to receive grace. Take some time and think about what grace means to you, but please don't ask why bad things happen to good people and good things happen to bad. This is only a perception and a trick; we do not know what is in anyone else's heart — that is between God and that person. You can, however, know what is in your own heart, and trust that *your* guardian angel is looking out after *you* and is God's assistant for providing the gift of grace in *your* life.

For more insight, look up the word *grace* in the dictionary. The *Oxford American Dictionary* defines it as:

1. the quality of being attractive, especially in movement, manner, or design. 2. elegance of manner, he had the grace to apologize, realized that this was right and proper, and did it. 3. favor, goodwill. 4. a delay or postponement granted as a favor, not as a right. 5. God's loving mercy toward mankind. 6. a short prayer of thanks before or after a meal.

Ask the angels to make you aware of the gift of grace, and to bring you into the nation of grace. Live in a state of grace in the nation of grace — in this world but not of it!

Practice 2: Perfect Timing

What on earth is perfect timing? Well, that is up to us individually to decide, but I think you know what I mean when I use the term. You especially know it when the angels are at play in your life. I think we have just as much to do with perfect timing as we do with luck. We can create it by dedicating our actions and decisions to the highest good, and opening ourselves to the right timing for changes to unfold gracefully in our lives. The way we do this is by consciously practicing patience. You have heard the saying "Patience is a virtue," and it is. Patience is calm endurance and wakeful consciousness.

Watch impatient people sometime and you will see them acting unconsciously and usually unconscientiously. Actions will take place that cause mishap for them and irritation for those around them. Impatient people are usually trying to avoid themselves and avoid being alone with themselves. To curb this tendency, practice anything that calms you and slows you down and keeps you in the moment, such as reading, meditation, cooking, hobbies, art, chopping wood, and carrying water. Patience has a negative connotation for some people; it probably takes them back in time when they were children and couldn't wait for something to happen in the future that would be much more fun than what was happening in the present, and the first stages of obsession were forming. Once again, this relates to our fear of being bored and is simply a choice of perception.

If you come upon a quiet day, without much action, be glad for the inner growth it provides. Don't think of it as negative; choose a quiet activity for a quiet day and regenerate for a more active time. Patience is creative, and it allows grace and right timing. Practice contemplation for decision making. Contemplation and patience can become key accelerators for a state of grace to occur in your life on earth, where you can be in this world (for enlightened service) but not of it. Ask the angels for perfect timing and patience to become effortless, and you will know how to live.

Practice 3: Stopping Wanting

When I stop to think about how many times I say, "I want such and such," or think to myself, "I want such and such," I am amazed. What a catch wanting something is; it takes me right out of the present and consumes my focus. Some wants are necessary, such as wanting a glass of water because we are thirsty and so forth. But when the wants get larger, they make us waste precious present time. For example, when I want a larger house, larger car, larger income, larger brain, and larger angels, what usually happens is that the wants keep getting larger even when I attain my larger "want goals." All this means is that wants are a time and a grace waster. Each time you hear yourself say, "I want this or that," either give up what you are wanting and be in the moment, or go get what you want if that is feasible. Try releasing your wants at least one a day, and see what happens. Ask the angels to take the desired want and replace it immediately with loving mental peace, and you will have everything you ever wanted!

Chapter 13

Understanding and Forgiveness

Do not weep; do not wax indignant. Understand.

Baruch Spinoza

Understand is an odd word, but I think most people are familiar with its nature. If you understand something, or stand under something, you have perceived the meaning or nature of whatever it is you understand. In essence, understanding means discernment—perceiving clearly with the mind and senses. With understanding comes patience and acceptance.

Most people are also familiar with the opposite experience of not perceiving clearly. Anger, fear, and misdirected actions can result. Angels help us greatly in the area of understanding. Our guardian angel is always with us and always has a clear view—void of emotional reaction—of any situation. Therefore, if we need insight into a situation, we can ask the angels for their take on the situation.

One way to get a clearer view of the world is to discover the emotions that cloud our perception, then work on releasing them. I believe anger can be the most dangerous cloud, especially when it is pent up and suppressed; then the top blows off suddenly. Fear is a dark cloud that dims our view. Pessimism or defensive negative attitudes color the world a dark gray. To clear the sky in our minds of these dark and gloomy clouds, we can practice becoming aware; we can practice understanding what storm front brought them our way. To do this takes practice.

Some of us have a problem understanding forgiveness. Forgiveness usually implies that a negative action took place and is causing one or more people to feel hurt and angry. By a negative action, I mean something that fits a concept of bad, horrible, spiteful, or intentionally hurtful. The unfortunate result of these judgments is a growing tension between the two or more parties involved. The tension is like a haze preventing total clarity. If something has happened to you that you find difficult or impossible to forgive, it is important that you examine the situation with the angels to get a clearer view. First of all, keep in mind that whatever the situation, it happened in the past. Every time you think about it, you are using valuable creative energy and precious present moments to focus your energy on the past.

I am going to make a strong statement: It is absolutely ridiculous and a waste of time to allow someone else's behavior to hurt you or bother you. If you are at a point where someone else's behavior is hurting you or bothering you, you are trying to control him or her. I'm sure everyone reading this can think of a million arguments to this. I can certainly think of behaviors people engage in that I don't like. But what do these behaviors really have to do with me? How did I get to a place where other people have the power to control my behavior, or where I think I have the right to control theirs? There are many ways we try to control our relationships with others. We may induce guilt, buy them things, change our behavior to match theirs, take care of them, and so forth. We engage in these patterns to try to create an illusion of security — someone/something outside ourselves to depend on. This would be nice, but it is much nicer when we can depend on ourselves for our own happiness.

This situation calls for balance. When we are close to someone, we have to be willing to accept and release that person at all times from a space of no rules and unconditional love. We can only achieve this state when we stay in a space of wisdom. In Chapter 9, I discussed the wise inner angel. Your wise inner angel is a great help with issues of control and forgiveness. Become one with your wise inner angel at the times when you feel unforgiving toward a person or situation. Take a look at things through the eyes of wisdom, and your perception is sure to change. All of this applies in the area of self-forgiveness. Forgiving yourself may be more difficult than forgiving others. So bring in the angels and release yourself from the bondage of guilt, shame, and self-hatred.

Practice 1: Clearing the Sky of Your Mind

The angels can help clear dark clouds from your mind. Take some deep breaths and imagine you are breathing in angel energy. It might help to imagine it has a fresh, minty scent. (If you want to get fancy, you can actually inhale an angelic aroma.) Angels exist in a realm of bright, clear light. In fact, their realm has been described as being so bright that human beings can hardly stand it for long. The light is white; white light is formed by the entire spectrum of color rays. When you take each deep breath, imagine this light penetrating all the circuits in your brain and blasting through blocked pathways.

If you ever find yourself in a state of catatonia (morbid gloom and depression), quickly take a deep breath and ask the angels to blast it away. Imagine all the gifts of the angels traveling to your brain — mirth, joyful abandonment, cheerfulness, humor, and glee. This may not have an immediate effect, since going with the change right away entails deep trust in the angels. It takes practice to reach this state quickly, but, enlightenment can happen in an instant with the angels, once you learn to open yourself to their help.

If you want to buy or devise an angelic inhaler, the field of aromatherapy can be helpful. Find two or three fragrances that make you feel good and whenever you need some daylight in your mind from the angels, inhale your chosen fragrances. As you breathe in the fragrances, ask the angels for understanding. If thoughts come to you that don't make too much sense at the moment, don't discard them. Keep a mental note or write the thoughts in your journal. These random thoughts can be very important at a later time. (But don't read too much into the thoughts either—strive for balance and clarity.)

Remember to breathe. Breathing is important at all times, even when you are feeling great. Breathe in and thank the angels for all of their gifts; they are as free as the air we breathe.

Practice 2: Forgiving and Blessing— The Actions of Release

Angels are forgiveness operators; they can make the connections for you if you are willing to forgive and release. Willingness is the key element here. Once you are truly willing to forgive and go on, the process of forgiveness has begun. To encourage willingness, first ask the angels for help, then begin to change your view of the aspects surrounding the situation. Think positively! Start to look at the bright side, because there definitely is one. If someone has disturbed, hurt, or attacked your mental peace, see this as the gift that it is. First of all, this experience allows you the opportunity to develop spiritual strength and virtue through forgiveness. Second, it brings change with it, which means something great is coming your way—as soon as you release the hurt.

If there are people you want to forgive who won't cooperate physically, forgive them in your mind. Mentally bless people who have disturbed you and thank them for the chance to cultivate your virtues. Whenever you think of them, send a beam of white angel light their way. If you start thinking negatively about them, finish the thought and then change it; release the thought, and set yourself free. Forgiveness takes practice, but it doesn't have to be overwhelming. Again, forgiveness entails the ability to control our emotional reaction and attitude toward life and people. Why become a prisoner of your own reactions and attitudes? Free yourself, forgive yourself, and forgive life for not always being easy.

Work with the angels to develop a brain program to enable you to detect the precise moment when your perceptions change from forgiveness to resentment. Work on releasing any thought that has to do with punishment or revenge toward others or yourself. This may seem difficult, but the angels will help you set up alarms in your mind, so that if a negative perception starts to take over, you will have the choice to stop it in its track. You will also find that when you give up the desire for revenge or superiority, you will be rewarded in many ways. Just trust and forgive. Release the past. We have a lot to do right now, and clinging to the past slows our progress!

Practice 3: Transmuting Anger

If you take the "r" off *anger* and replace it with an "l," you get *angel.* That doesn't make anger any more attractive, but with a little angelic understanding you'll have an easier time transmuting and dealing with anger. I've discussed the issue of anger with many people, and most agree that anger is somewhat mysterious because no matter what you do, it seems at times almost impossible to get rid of. Anger is one of those reactions that can appear again long after you thought you were finished dealing with it. Our culture and many others seem to find anger a confusing issue. For example, we may have been stopped many times when beginning to express our anger as children; then psychotherapists tell us as adults that suppressing our anger leads to illness and depression and all sorts of other unpleasant things. The messages regarding anger are definitely mixed and confusing.

I would imagine that most people have a story of when they "blew their top" and did something wild in response to their anger. I know I have a few. The moment when we lose control can make the situation we are dealing with a lot worse.

I've also noted that anger is not a set emotion in people; anger seems to take on different degrees with different people. For example, if you think about all the people you have known, you could most likely come up with someone who is angry all the time. Everything that happens seems to set this person off. You could also think of someone who hardly ever stays angry and who has a very loving and positive nature most of the time. Our perceptions of a situation rule our emotional response. So a person with a positive and optimystic attitude tends to perceive a situation in a less angry way. In contrast, almost everything angry people experience may be interpreted as an injustice, provocation, or an attack on their personalities. These are two extreme examples, but in the case of any emotion response we do have a degree of choice in how we are going to react.

Again, the art of awareness is important. When you feel angry, there is a reason. To deal with anger, you must first look at the obvious facts. Listen to yourself when you are expressing anger to a friend or when you are writing down your feelings. Examine what you are saying. Next, use your intuition to trace the origins of your angry feelings. There may well be people around you who for some reason or another (don't take it personally — it's their problem) are undermining your good nature. If you find this to be the case, just remain aware and ask your angel to speak to theirs regarding the matter; then protect yourself with the angels' light. Shine it out to them, and their attacks won't be able to get through the light. The trick is to become aware and to see the situation without emotional attachments.

Also ask yourself whether the situations you are angry about are really your problem. I know I have the tendency to react angrily to situations where there is an underdog; I often want to go take care of the problem. This is especially difficult when children are involved. We have to keep in mind that anger clouds our thinking. There are many good reasons to feel anger these days. Just watch the news in an angry mood and soon you will be ready to explode. So keep your mind clear and work on not taking things personally. Keep your center strong and protected in the light. The angels are with you, and they always have a clear perception. So align yourself with your guardian angel and open yourself to a clear understanding of the situation. Anger is like gasoline, always waiting to ignite; all it needs is a lighted match thrown on it in the form of a reaction.

With the help of the angels, I have found I have a better perspective on the issue of anger. Be sure not to take anger out on yourself. Think of ways to deal with it constructively. One time, while working with a group of junior high students, a girl in the group mentioned that at times she felt like committing suicide. Instead of reacting emotionally to the seriousness of her statement, I said, "Yes, I would imagine everyone in the room has felt so much anger about life that they have turned it toward themselves and thought about suicide." I then asked the group to share some constructive ways to work out their anger instead of turning it inward. They had some great suggestions, such as talk to a counselor or a friend (someone you trust), call a hot-line, write a poem, hit your pillow, scream and cry into your pillow, write all your feelings in a journal, write a letter to someone but don't send it, draw pictures of your feelings, take a walk and cool off, listen to music, exercise or dance rigorously, and think of positive things. Then they did something really wonderful; all of them in their own unique ways offered to be this girl's friend, showing her love in their own special ways. The change in her was 180 degrees; she went from being very closed off, sad, and angry to being very open, alive, fun, and loving. And that is what angels are all about! Angels are there for you; they are your hotline to call on anytime, they are your friends to tell if no one else is around, and most of all they are waiting to show you love in their own special way, to free you to be fully alive and to be happy you are you.

Part Five

Let Go and Let the Angels

About Part Five:

Attachment and Noncontingency

You may have had the experience of wanting something so much that it consumed your every moment. Time was spent visualizing, praying, manifesting, asking, role playing, energizing the image—in other words doing everything you could think of to bring your ideal into existence. So you did all this work, and nothing really materialized. Then one day you decided to give it up, to surrender, to detach, and to release; lo and behold, just when you had stopped the wanting, what you wished for came your way!

Angels would like us to reach a state of nonattachment, simply because attachments weigh us down and give us a tendency to overreact to situations. Why do we react? What happens when we lose control of our emotions? Emotional reactions can get us in trouble. To have an emotional response to something means we have invested part of ourselves and formed an attachment to a certain outcome. When the desired outcome doesn't happen, we overreact. We may be shocked, angered, or saddened.

Think of a time you were stressed out and off your center. Maybe you were in a hurry and something spilled or got knocked over and you reacted as if it were the worst thing imaginable. This is actually very funny and an example of taking ourselves way too seriously. Overreacting can be a result of either being too stressed out or being too invested in something. Both situations entail heaviness and struggle. To stop overreacting takes time and practice. The first step is just to become more aware of what you are doing.

Nonattachment is the ultimate discipline for living fully in the present. Attachments make us heavy and bound to earth. When we release ourselves from the seriousness of life attachments, we soar to the heights of angelic bliss and humor. Attachments form in many ways. We are attached to people, places, and things. When these people, places, and things don't cooperate with our expectations, we experience fear, separation anxiety, and conflicts (just to name a few). Learning to release and detach, even in a small way, frees our spirits; with the help of the angels, it isn't as difficult as we may think.

One approach to untangling the knot of attachment is to develop the attitude of "noncontingency." Contingency means that one thing depends upon another. A caused B. In order to get to B, you must get to A first. Having B depends on having A. Noncontingency means that B does not necessarily depend on A.

The belief that B necessarily depends on A becomes especially insidious if B happens to be something essential for your health, happiness, or ability to perform. For example, you may tell yourself that your happiness depends on something (A). Then you are really sunk, because A may be something you cannot control, or, even worse, something you can have only if you are in a good state of mind to begin with.

The attitude of noncontingency can serve you well. Noncontingency means that you systematically reject your beliefs in contingency. And, after all, how can you know that your favorite B is necessarily dependent on some unattainable A? It might actually depend on something you have never even thought of, or on nothing at all.

Noncontingency is one of the most powerful mental attitudes you can assume. It puts you above your limited beliefs, into the realm of the higher self that can rise above the limitations of who you think you are at the moment. The angels exist in this realm, because they see you for who you really are.

People who practice noncontingency often find it is correlated with bliss — and vice versa — that is, those who have approached the states of bliss and nonattachment through yogic practices, meditation, isolation, or even biofeedback find that an attitude of noncontingency accompanies bliss, along with the feeling of unlimited possibilities. This is the state of power and possibilities beyond the confines of the known world. It is the entry gate to what esoteric philosophy calls the "causal plane," because it is the real cause of everything that appears to go on in the world of so-called cause and effect.

Chapter 14

Let the Angels Carry You

Ultimately, if we dropped all of our human baggage, we would be light enough to fly with the angels. This may not seem like a reasonable quest, because we are humans and some baggage goes along with the human experience. However, as you know, we always have the choice to drop the baggage that weighs too much, and we can do this by turning it over to the angels. My friend Jai described her life, her path, as walking on a tightrope. The higher you get (with less and less baggage), the more joy, love, and peace you attain. There is one glitch; the higher you are, the farther you have to fall. If you are afraid of heights, don't worry, because if you put your trust in God and surrender, if and when you do occasionally fall, there is a safety net to catch you — the angels. When they catch you, they may decide to carry you for a while or fly you right back up; all you have to do is trust them, because it is all okay.

Have you ever given a thought to who is in control of your life? Usually people are divided on this issue. Some people think they control what happens to them, and others think they are at the mercy of external events with no control over what happens to them. People are said to have an external locus of control when they believe that what happens to them is more controlled by external sources and forces than by their own actions. On the other hand, those who perceive themselves as in charge of their own lives have an internal locus of control, and they believe their actions make a difference. They realize that they may not be able to control all external events, but they know that they can control their reactions to events.

The effects of both types of control show themselves most distinctly when people become seriously ill or injured. People with an external focus of control feel at the mercy of doctors, loved ones, and negative circumstances. Having an internal locus of control gives people the ability to take charge of their healing and influence circumstances positively. The long-range health prognosis is far better for people with an internal locus of control.

There are basically two kinds of problems we face. One kind of problem arises from the random functioning of the universe. Natural disasters such as earthquakes or hurricanes are situations we don't have individual control over. The other kind of problem is the kind we create ourselves; such problems arise from an attempt to manipulate or control our environment and the circumstances or people around us. Wouldn't it be nice if we really could control everyone around us? We know what is best; we know if only our spouse, our children, and our coworkers would just do what we think they should everything would run smoothly. Unless you are an enlightened master, you are trying to control someone or some situation prevalent in your life. Your type of control may be very subtle, or it may be very loud. The desire to control is definitely part of human nature! Needing to control causes problems because it is impossible to make people and situations that surround you do exactly what you want. When we lose control over a situation, we feel life is not manageable. When we realize we hold the power to control how we react to life and how we feel about ourselves, then our own lives becomes manageable.

Increasing happiness and self-love is in our power regardless of circumstances. By giving over our external control to a loving higher power (the angels), we gain internal control that is based on trust and self-love. Life is really more fun when we give up the need to control. It seems risky at times, but the situations you attract by not needing to control allow you true freedom. The angels are with us on this one. They know how tempted we are by the issue of control. It comes with the territory of free will. Replace the word *control* with the word *trust* in your vocabulary; then sit back and watch the show.

Practice 1: What Is the Essence of Your Higher Power?

We create our own experience of God's love through the gift of free will. If we create a loving and forgiving God who works with loving angels, then we've created a support system we can trust in. We can trust the higher power in our lives to take over situations that torment us and keep us from living happily. Think about what kind of higher power you have created in your life. Think back on times when you had to ask or rely on your higher power for help: What happened? Did you feel safe and taken care of inside, or did a wave of fear sweep over you?

When you do something you have judged "bad," do you punish yourself by feeling guilty and bringing on a negative event, or does some force that you feel you have no control over come in and spank you with negativity? Either way, you do the punishing, just as you commit the act for which you feel a need to punish yourself. This idea may conflict with religious belief systems some people grew up with, but consider it regardless of your belief system. The world can be frightening enough by itself. And, when we make heaven a place of righteous, strict judgments, where do we find solace?

When we believe that heaven is on our side, our worldly life will be colored in lighter shades. This is not that difficult to achieve. But it takes ignoring some of the ugliness and focusing only on the beautiful. Take a moment; the beauty is all around you. Listen for the song of a bird; regardless of your surroundings, there are birds nearby. Watch the sky; notice the colors of the sun as it sets or rises. Take a walk in a park, study a tree, and smell the flowers. Ask the angels to take you on a tour of the beautiful. Watch children play. Listen to beautiful music. Forget the rest of the world; the powers of heaven are here on earth — all we need to do is focus our attention on beauty. Make finding beauty part of your daily life, and focus your attention on beauty for at least a little while each day. The angels will reward you.

If you need to lighten up the essence of your higher power, by all means do it. One way to do this is by cultivating abundance, by envisioning the divine as a higher power who is more than enough — more than we could ever ask for. If we ask, we are given more. Get in touch with the abundance of love heaven has surrounded you with. The divine is expansive and moving, and it would be foolish to define in strict terms. Go beyond descriptions and definitions. Tap into the divine, expansive consciousness that frees your soul with abundance. As you slowly refocus and lighten up, and allow the essence of heaven into your life, your attitude will undergo change. You will feel powerful and protected in a natural way, and the true gifts of the angelic world will come your way. And never forget about divine humor. When challenging "bad" things happen, stand back with your higher self, the angels, and the divine higher power and have a good laugh together.

Practice 2: Surrendering External Control

Relax for a moment and give some thought to whether your locus of control is mostly internal or mostly external. Ask yourself some questions. What has life taught you about control up to this point? Do you feel more like a victim of the wrath of the universe, or like a strong player in the game? Think of something that went wrong in your life that you didn't plan for. Did you have complete control over the situation, or feel completely helpless? When something went wrong, did you turn to a higher power for inner strength, or give up and feel cheated? Maybe you are someone who does both. Maybe it depends on the situation. The point is we often don't know; that is, we don't often sit back and think about the issue of control. So before something major happens to you, give some thought to control. Take this process lightly. This issue can get a little heavy, and you wouldn't want that to happen!

Control is a seductive illusion; it is a trick played on our minds. At times we may use extreme self-reliance as a defense. We are so in control of ourselves that we think: Who needs anyone else? Who even needs God? If we believe strongly in our own power to control outcomes, then the world will be safe and manageable, right? Wrong, because the fact is we really do not have complete control over what happens to us. We have a certain amount of influence, but ultimately we cannot direct the tides. Begin to learn about your own locus of control, and give the angels external control so that you can develop an internal locus of control based on trust and self-love.

Think of some issues in your life that could use a little angelic surrender magic. The issue could be big or small, human or nonhuman. Make a list of these issues, then declare them the property of the angels. You no longer own or are fully responsible for them. You are surrendering them to the angels. Ask the angels to sprinkle some magic on them, and trust that everything will work out for your highest good and that of the universe. If you want to, you can use your imagination and visualize some of the magic. Just don't get attached to outcomes; always leave room for the angels to spread their wings and do their magic.

Be inspired. Read a book or see a movie about someone's victory over life's hardships. Look for a spiritual theme. Check for locus of control. Look for self-esteem. Figure out what inspires you about the story or what doesn't. Would you do things differently? Could you handle it? Was the character weak at times? What kept him or her going? Think about the inspiring book or movie often if it had a positive effect on you, and each time you think of it give up a problem you have. Simply refuse to acknowledge the problem anymore; see it as meaningless compared to your goals and aspirations. Ask the angels to be with you whenever hardships run you aground.

Practice 3: Being Carried Away by the Angels

For this practice, you may want to put on some music that makes you feel as if you are flying. Go into angel alpha state, and visualize and feel the angels carrying you. Start to experience the lightness and the humor of their realm. Your mood will instantly lighten up. Think of a place you want to fly over. Imagine that you are flying with the angels, and if you like, imagine you are one of them. Maybe you are flying over a beautiful forest, maybe a lake. Use your imagination. Maybe you're high above a city at night admiring the glittering lights.

Fly for a while and then begin to see your life below. What does it look like from so high up? Is it funny? Sad? Interesting? Think about whether or not you are carrying any unwanted baggage with you on this flight. If you are, ask the angels to transmute it, to help you get rid of it. Now be yourself again. You are still flying with the angels, but they are carrying you. You have landed on the top of a beam of light. You must stay centered or you will begin to fall. If you feel yourself falling, surrender to the angels; they are your safety net and will be there to catch you. When you stand on top of this light beam, you are one with your full empowerment. You are one with the universe; you have cosmic consciousness. There is no past and no future — just now. Experience this for a while and allow yourself to go wherever you need to; just be sure to stay with the angels. After a while, come out of angel alpha and feel your center of gravity come into alignment here on the earth. Remember the experience and call up the vision whenever you are entering uncharted territory and feel unsure of yourself.

Chapter 15

Changing Work to Play

Many great teachers, religious or otherwise, have walked the Earth, and from each one we can learn. Yet the angels, from their vantage point and from their interplay with our consciousness, can see what we truly are, can see the steps in front of us, and continue to help us connect to our divine origin and goal. Now we can consciously seek their cooperation.

Dorothy Maclean

I often hear people say how hard they are working and what slow progress they are making. When we work, too often we force. Force in any situation ends up setting us back and often blocking the way of abundance. Trusting the angels and allowing most of our work to take place in the unseen realm of heaven will bring us more than what we need. A willingness to release the struggle will make us more creative in what we do. Angels help us attract situations into our life to help us be our best possible selves.

If I'm not careful, I find myself using the word *work* way too often. I use it to represent my responsibilities, and the problem with that is that it puts a negative projection out. Therefore, I may not be as creative and happy when I am actually doing the "work." There really is no reason to work. Again, it is all in our attitude; if we want, we can change our work into play. And, once again, angels are our role models for turning work to play, because all they do is play and dance with the divine flow of the universe. We can flow with the divine also, and our lives will be happier and much more creative. All it takes is a little bit of angel fun.

When discussing work, we cannot dismiss the idea of having a job. Think about your job, if you have one. Do you like it? If not, do you like to complain about it? Whatever your job is, you can find some positive aspects to it. If you are bored with your job, bring in some new energy—the angels. The way to do this is to stay focused on the positive and think of some new ways of being at your job. The angels will help you, and pretty soon you may find yourself very playful and creative on the job. If you are out of a job and are finding yourself idle, this can feel worse than working at a job you think you hate. But, again, it doesn't have to be negative; bring in the angels and have some fun with all that idle time. When you clean your house, pretend you are a child playing house. Play some music. Listen to something by Mozart or to any music that is alive and spirited. As you do your chores, dance and be childlike and silly. The angels will join in quickly and bring joy to whatever you are doing.

We get joy directly from the angels. If you are feeling joy, you are feeling the angels. There is no separation. Joy and mirth are angelic inventions designed to give us humans a break from the mundane. Joy and mirth are like true happiness; we cannot pay for them or pursue them intently. Their visits are spontaneous; we may never know when or where we will receive joy and mirth. We can only make ourselves more available to receiving the gifts of joy and mirth, by keeping our minds open and flexible—in other words, spontaneous and childlike.

The quotation at the beginning of this chapter means a lot to me personally. In my mind, it sums up the most important reasons for connecting with angels. A lifetime is a process of awakening to who you really are, and the angels know you well. The angels hold you in a projection of your highest self and your highest intentions/gifts for this lifetime. The angels want to connect you to your divine origin, and they want to dance and play with your consciousness — making you light and happy. When you find your life's play with the angels' help, you will be happy without reason, right here and right now. This in turn will magnetize all sorts of joyful, mirthful, and wonderful happenings your way.

Practice 1: Cultivating Patience and Discipline

Patience and discipline can be a lot of fun. You may doubt this, but it is true. Patience is a form of calmness. Think of something that tries your patience. Now imagine yourself standing back in this situation with a pleasant look on your face, just watching. Look for humor; it is most likely involved. There may be many situations each day that make you impatient, for example, waiting on a phone line for your call to go through, or waiting in line, or getting stuck in traffic, and so forth. Cultivate some creative patience and calm in these little situations. Start to daydream about amusing and wonderful things. Use the time to discuss your life with the angels; this will change your mood and may even make you laugh hysterically. Start to identify patience with play and humor. The angels will help you; they have all the time in the world to play with you.

Discover what makes you impatient; note what you are waiting for to enable you to relax. List all the things you can think of that will make you happier if and when they happen. Now realize that happiness comes from within, and you cannot depend on other situations or other people to bring you happiness. If you create happiness within yourself, it is yours regardless of what may come. Goals we set for ourselves do not come with impatience in the package. Impatience is something we create when we are not flexible in our thinking.

You may be thinking that if only you had more discipline in your life you could accomplish great things. Well, why not get some? Become a disciple of the angels, and discipline will be fun. When you discover your life's play, what you are all about, discipline won't be so difficult — especially if you make the concept positive!

Practice 2: Freeing Your Inner Angel Child

Changing the concept of work is easier when we reintroduce ourself to our inner angel child. The inner angel child is your higher self — the pure and unadulterated essence of *you*. The human spirit is childlike and joyful. But the human spirit is very vulnerable. It needs protection in the form of love to grow and strengthen in a positive way. Many human spirits have been broken and repressed along the way through childhood and adolescence into adulthood. We may need to go within and rebirth our inner child so we can integrate joy and love back into our human spirits.

Visualize a happy child. The one thing that comes to my mind right away is joy — one of the angel's inventions specifically designated for humans. Children transmit joy easily — without effort — just by being themselves in the moment. At one time, we were pure joy transmitters, which means we were fully integrated with the angels. We can become fully integrated with the angels once again by allowing joy to flow freely in our lives. This again brings us back to *play*, the divine play of creation. Playing is the ultimate act of being in the moment. Forget work; take the word out of your mind and replace it with play. This won't be easy, but it will be worthwhile.

One of the basic themes of this book is to free your inner child and integrate the spirit of child joy into your being. This will ultimately make you a whole person, because by rediscovering your child essence, you discover who you truly are. The angels can play very well with an integrated human; the path is open and clear and the angels can guide without stodgy adult emotional blocks or a tendency to complicate everything. I was once accused of being too simplistic after an angel talk. I took this as a compliment. I am quite content with my level of intelligence, and I usually do not feel the need to prove it to anyone. I also believe in simplicity versus complexity. Why take the beautiful, joyful, life-affirming message that the angels are here to make us happier, and complicate it with a bunch of unnecessary tricks, words, and belief systems? Forget it. I say let go of this ridiculous notion of being an adult! It is the leading cause of spirit death among people over the age of twelve. Be yourself — which means be one with your child within — and transmit some joy to those stodgy adults who want everything to be so serious and complicated.

The following poem is from a very special book called *Look Upon the Children,* written by Ken Cousens. I love poetry, but I often find it to be too far removed from the reader's consciousness. Ken's poetry book is different, in part because we all share a common experience — we were all children at one time. Ken has skillfully captured childhood in a universal and timeless way. With his permission, I offer you a further chance to connect with your inner angel child.

A Child's Season

A spring song of laughter
Is a child's season
Touching flowers, singing rain
Each fragrant petal
Each green grass stain
Drifting hours with no reason
Napping after a nonsense game

Summer's heat
Is a child's call

Silver fish in waterfall
Each taste of life on wind carefree
Popsicles for you and me
Splash and shout, cold delight
Daddy's hand and starlit night

Autumn's colors
Are a child's dream
Windy leaves, dancing waifs
Broken toys along the way
Pumpkins smile, scary scenes
Make believe and Halloween
All a part of child's play

Winter's cold
A child's cozy time
Snuggle warm and hot chocolate
Reading, drawing, growing minds
Story time we can't forget
Each year we grow but no wonder yet
Our love is strong as life unwinds

Season's spin, whirling top
Years unfold, no time to stop
A child's season we all sustain
We come and go but life remains
Love our best is all we're told
And the child inside will thus unfold

Ken Cousens

Practice 3: Child of Light

No matter what human age you are, you are a *child*. In Chapter 1, I talked about each of us having a special color of the light of God. This light we possess is our gift for the world, and when it shines brightly our essence is transmitted and our gift is received. In this light of God, we are always children. The light is eternally ours. The light is within us and needs clear windows to shine brightly through. Light can dim. When we are depressed and unhappy, we have dimmed our light; we have repressed it. Too often, the pressures of adulthood dim our light and to get it back we must get back to our true light nature as children of God and light.

While you read this, do a light body check. We will start with your feet: Where are they positioned, and what are they doing? Wiggle them around, and allow light to enfold them. How about your legs? Are they crossed? Are they straight or bent? How do they feel? Allow the light into your legs and feel it open channels of flexibility to keep the light alive. Are your hands comfortable and loose or tensed up as you hold the book? Are your arms heavy, light, bent? Bring in the light and visualize your arms as wings of light, ready to fly at a moment's notice. Now focus on your center, the area of your body where organs do chemistry experiments and your heart pumps blood energy to all parts of your body. Take a deep breath and loosen up all the muscles in your stomach. Loosen up your shoulders. Wiggle and push as if you were a baby chick escaping from its birth egg. Take another breath, this time of pure light.

Now comes the tough part. Relax your mind, which most likely feels like it is in your head. Relax your neck muscles, stretch them gently, and feel your neck disappear. Your head is now suspended in space. What do you see, hear, smell, and taste? Relax the muscles in your face. Let your mind run free for a moment, and then bring it into focus for a few checkpoints of your present consciousness.

What are you acting like? What is the prevailing tone of your life lately? Are you acting like an adult plagued by responsibilities that no one could ever understand or help you with? If so, remember that you are a child of light; as you learn to play with the divine flow of life, responsibilities are changed to games. Start to figure out how your little dissatisfactions project themselves in your life. If you are worrying about something, realize that worry is not a child of light problem, so give it over to the angels. If you are experiencing low energy, ask the angels to help you rediscover your child of light energy. Sadness or depression means the light is dim, and the adult in you has had it and turned down the light so you won't hurt anymore. Be a child of light and reconnect with the joy of light childhood. Turn the light back on and allow it to shine brightly; the angels are here to help! Ask for some joy to replace the sadness.

Are you basically happy? Know inside if you are it is not because of that wonderful new toy you have or that great job you got or the wonderful relationship you have with another person. The happiness you are feeling is because you love yourself and allowed nice happenings to come your way. If the circumstances changed or left, you would still have this happiness. Because happiness comes from within, and all children of light know how to be one with the essence of happiness. How friendly are you? Do you allow people to be themselves and come and go in your life? A child of light is friendly and attracts friendly and magical people. The above are just some questions to ask yourself and may allow greater awareness and insight into areas of your life where you want the light to shine more brightly.

This exercise is not meant to be taken seriously. It is simply a checkpoint for you to focus your attention on the child of light that you are. We don't always remember that we are a child of light and that we have a nurturing parent — the ever-loving higher power in the universe, maintained and made personal to us through and by the angels — who can take care of problems that are not really ours. All we need to do is remember to give over our adult problems to be solved for the highest good in the universe, *to let go and let the angels.*

Chapter 16

Freedom

A great many people think they are thinking when they are merely rearranging their prejudices.

William James

Are you a "free" person? Are you a "freethinker"? Consider these points (from the definition of *free* in the *Oxford American Dictionary*) on the issue of being free, then decide. One, if you are free you are not a slave and are not under the power of others. Two, if you are free you have private rights that are respected, and you are not controlled by a despotic government. Three, if you are free you are not fixed or held down, restricted, or controlled by rules. You are not subject to or affected by any negative influence, that is, you are "free from blame." Four, if you are free, you are without payment — in other words, you don't have a price. Five, if you are free, you are free of appointments or things to do and you give of your time freely. This may give you a beginning idea of how free you are — or aren't.

Now please don't start worrying about freedom. True freedom of spirit may take a lifetime to achieve. If you want to be freer in your thinking and your life-style, examine the situations in your life and belief system that keep you from expressing yourself as a free individual. In essence, find out what keeps you from true freedom and eliminate your shackles.

Freedom is important to the angels, which means they will be on your side in your quest for freedom. The angels are free from the serious situations humans must face daily, but they know we humans need balance in our lives. We have serious issues in our lives, but we also have the power to rise above them and have fun as often as we like. We can free ourselves to be childlike and spontaneous; we can attract interesting and unusual circumstances that will make life much more exciting. If we take ourselves lightly and lighten our baggage, we are free to move quickly down the river of life and welcome change. The world seems to move so fast now that it is of paramount importance for us to be lighter and freer.

A major weight in our lives is our constant need to compare and judge. Even the word *judgment* is heavy and conjures up the image of the scales of justice or a judgment that is harsh and heavy. If we don't judge and compare, we do not need scales. Another heavy weight is fixed opinions, or strong opinions that we hold onto for dear life. The problem with opinions is that they carry the issue of right and wrong, which is totally unnecessary. Why does one opinion need to be right and another wrong? We all have different experiences of life and so we will all have different versions of life — different or varied, but not right or wrong. And where on earth have you gotten these opinions? Are they really yours or have you formed them from teachers, books, T.V., and so forth? Or, worse, you may be reciting verbatim someone else's opinion. Some people are so convinced of their own opinions that they go out and kill others who they perceive have the wrong opinions. Opinions can be dangerous!

Belief systems are also very confining, and very tricky. We may think we have a belief system in which we are totally free, but the two don't go together. In essence, true freedom is a lot like true happiness. That is, happiness and freedom really exist only in our minds. They have nothing to do with what we have or where we live; they depend on how we think of these things, on our attitude toward life's situations. As always, remember that this book is based on my opinions and attitudes toward life and angels. So take only what you want from it, what feels freeing to you. I am not claiming to be right; I am only following a path I believe will free me individually so that my days will be happier and my nights lighter—a life path that the angels will bless with their light and joy.

Practice 1: Loosening the Grip of a Belief System

I have always liked the term *freethinker,* mainly because it fits my belief system about myself. The problem with a belief system is that it is not conducive to free thinking. Even if you believe you are free, that belief is restraining because it may color your behavior in some way so that your behavior isn't really free from your thoughts or beliefs.

Conflicts arise when our belief systems don't fit our experiences, and when others refuse to fit our beliefs. We may have a belief about what marriage is, for example, but our experience of it may be completely different, so a conflict materializes. We may have a belief about the way we and others should be treated, and when it doesn't happen that way sparks may fly. Our belief system may tell us to not eat animal flesh, so when others do we consider them wrong.

Think about a belief system you may have, and start to loosen its boundaries. If it is a really strict one, get out the dynamite and blast it apart. This takes some courage because a lot of us believe that without our rules and beliefs we would be nothing and life would be chaos. Remember that with the angels on our side we are guided upward, and some of our beliefs are too heavy to go with us to the top. These coming days, months, and years are going to be very interesting and very fast. We have no need for extra weight in the form of strict beliefs. Free your thinking now. The angels are with you on this one; you don't need all of those rules! Trust yourself and know yourself; then you will know the angels, and you will know how to live by the moment.

Practice 2: Ceasing Comparing, Labeling, and Judging

Since everything is but an apparition,
perfect in being what it is,
having nothing to do with good or bad,
acceptance or rejection,
one may well burst out in laughter.

Long-Chen-Pa

Freedom begins where judging ends. We humans judge and compare everything all day long, even in our sleep. We judge other people, we judge inanimate objects, we judge our own experiences and those of others, and we constantly judge ourselves. Seeing each day's experiences as fascinating, interesting, and challenging, instead of good, bad, or just like such and such, frees us to live in the moment and be more effective at solving the problems we face. People are not bad. Sometimes they may not behave the way we would like them to, but this has nothing to do with them as a whole. People are not good or bad. Situations are not good or bad. Objects are not good or bad. If we cease comparing everything to something else or someone else in our lives, we will truly be free to see with the eyes of our inner angel child. Life is fascinating, and every day is like a vacation — offering a chance to explore new places. We need to free ourselves from the weight of judging and comparing everything that happens to us.

Think of a situation in your life that is bothering you, then ask yourself some questions. Have you already decided it is bad? If so, why is it bad in your mind? What are you comparing it to in your past that makes you believe it is bad? When you decide that a situation is good or bad, you leave no room for change or surprises. Life is dynamic; the very essence of life is movement, a changing of forms. When we label a moment, it becomes frozen into a single projection. If you look at a situation with your eyes and mind free of a set projection, you will see its true dynamics. The dynamics are vibrating and alive—ready to change at any moment and impossible to judge.

Moods are another facet of our lives that we label. Everyone knows what I mean if I say, "I'm in a bad mood; don't talk to me about that." Moods originate in our minds and can have a lot to do with the physical state of our bodies, and with our brain chemistry. When you declare yourself to be in a bad mood, you have already prolonged a temporary state. This, too, shall pass. You may be ready to come out of the bad mood, but others around you are still reinforcing your first conviction. Moods get all sorts of labels: bad/good, silly/serious, funny/sad, strange/normal. I'm sure you can come up with even more labels. Next time you start to define a mood, change directions and learn to just be and accept the moment. You don't need to explain yourself. Life is fast, and we cannot keep up with it if we stick ourselves in the mud of moods and frozen states of being.

To move away from strict comparisons and judgments, make a list of some words that better describe circumstances, people, and events in your life. Words such as fascinating, interesting, and amusing are fun words that can replace the good-or-bad, black-or-white syndrome. Eventually, you will want to lead yourself away from any type of label, but to wean yourself start with words that present a positive view and choose words that are not frozen. Pick a day and put the substitute words to use. Step back and view each situation you encounter with your angels. Ask the angels to give you new vision, to see life with fascination. First, always find the humor and laugh; the angels will help you with this. You may need to laugh to yourself in private, just in case those around you are taking things too seriously. Now pick one or two of your replacement words. Or, if you are ready to, don't use any words at all; just watch. While you are watching, experiment with a continuous state of release — release judgments and release reactions. One key is to depersonalize. Reach a state of divine indifference. This takes some practice, but angels dwell here, so they will be of great help. Imagine you are standing with your guardian angels and viewing life as an innocent bystander. By doing this, you will develop a calm center. When something truly challenging happens in your presence, you will act from your highest center. This is a practice in detachment.

When you have a thought from the past that seems unpleasant or makes you anxious in any way, view it differently. Go into angel alpha state and take away the labels of the past. If there is someone you think is "bad," be more specific. Find out what behavior it is that you didn't particularly like and depersonalize it. Realize the behavior had nothing to do with you personally. Your reaction may have caused you to believe it did, but now is the time to release your reaction. If people are truly putting forth the effort to hurt you, they can only succeed if you let them or if you react to them (I am talking about mental hurting, not physical).

Many of us tend to personalize everything; we think too much about ourselves. When something unpleasant happens, we might say, "I don't know what it is about me; I just seem to attract the same horrible situations. There must be something about my personality that other people can't handle." This occurs because we're comparing everything that happens to us to a situation in the past and so we form a pattern for ourselves that allows little room for change, regardless of circumstances. We have already compared, judged, and handed out the sentence. This also happens when we complete or compare ourselves to a close friend. Our individual lives are all unprecedented. Our relationships are unique. Sometimes, by putting lots of effort into analyzing our lives, we make comparisons. There may well be some truth in these comparisons, but in reality each situation stands on its own, and each experience we have is ours alone.

Each lesson we learn is for us; that is why it is impossible to really learn from someone else's mistakes.

The angels want to bring you to a state free from comparisons, labels, or judgments that tend to detract from being fully yourself. Being yourself is not the easiest task in the world. It seems easier to explain and compare ourselves to others' experiences and lives. This is one reason movies and television shows are so popular. We want to know in some way that we are just like other people, or that our problems are nothing compared to theirs. When you choose to live your life with angel consciousness, you have to trust that everything is perfect in being what it is. The angels may guide you in much different directions from your friends or from those people on T.V. You are charting a course never before taken, so get ready to burst out laughing at each turn you take; the angels are with you.

Part Six

Go Out and Love Some More

About Part Six:

Living a Spiritual Life

This part of the book is about getting out there in the world and living a spiritual but practical human life. It's not about doing religious service or going to church, but about really living fully. This will of course look different for each person. Learning to live with each other harmoniously is a noble cause. I call this process becoming an angel warrior.

In the final chapter, Angel Extras, you will learn about additional resources to encourage your ongoing relationship with the angels and to bring love and laughter into your life.

Chapter 17

Becoming an Angel Warrior

*The key to warriorship and the first principle of Shambhala
vision is not being afraid of who you are. Shambhala vision
teaches that in the face of the world's great problems we can
be heroic and kind at the same time. Shambhala vision is the
opposite of selfishness. When we are afraid of ourselves and
afraid of the seeming threat the world presents, then we
become extremely selfish. We want to build our own little
nests, our own cocoons, so that we can live by ourselves in
a secure way.*

Chogyam Trungpa,
Shambhala, The Sacred Path of the Warrior

All spiritual and personal growth practices run a risk of becoming self-indulgent unless we take our light and offer it to others unconditionally for their own transformation. World peace starts with personal peace and the practices of compassion, love, and respect for one another. The angels have a call out for warriors who are willing to stay awake and light the way with love and compassion for their fellow humans. In the Tibetan and Native

American traditions, a warrior is "one who is brave or fearless." Angel warriors have to be brave enough to stay awake and trust their hearts and trust the angels.

This book could also have been called *A Practical Guide to the Art of Angel Warriorship.* As with any art form, practice brings one closer to greatness, to being at one with the art. Our world is changing fast, and the challenge to remain peaceful and loving in the face of upheaval is an opportunity for greatness. We are bigger than we think; we are not just physical bodies in a physical reality with so many limitations. With the strength of the angels behind us, we are shape shifters who can shift into any form and go where we are needed. Angel warriorship is not about imposing our opinions onto others or rescuing others. And it is of course not about fighting or war; it is about peace. Terry Cole-Whittaker said something in a lecture I attended that is important to remember: "Peace is not boring!" Angel warriorship is about becoming a bright light that sends out love beams to transform the darkness of limitations, allowing us to fully realize our higher purpose and act from our inner wisdom. That is the true essence of peace.

Angel warriors know that in order to help the world become a happier and more peaceful place they must *know* that the experience of human life is basically good. Human life is basically humorous and beautiful. Many lovely and wonderful things happen every day around us and through us. Take moments during the day to honor the beauty of life. Honor the divine humor and the irony of human life presented to us every day: Learn to "expect the unexpected." Angel warriors are purveyors of *hope.*

Archangels

Archangels in all the holy books of the world are equally respected as being highly advanced emissaries intent on fulfilling missions entrusted to them by their Creator-God. They continually receive endowments of supernal energy with which to execute their tasks.

Flower A. Newhouse

We can call on particular archangels to help us strengthen and empower our angel warriorship. You can think of archangels as major angel archetypes, similar to the gods and goddesses of Greek and Roman mythology. As you think about your spiritual path, you may notice the influence of one or two archangels. If we discover areas in our lives where we could use the help of other archangels, we can call the energy of these angels to us by learning more about their special missions.

MICHAEL
(FROM THE HEBREW *MIKHA'EL*,
WHICH MEANS "WHO IS GOD?")

In the past three years, I have come across some very interesting information about the archangel Michael. Michael is known to most as the archangel who battles evil and cleanses people and places of discord and evil. Michael challenges humans who hold evil or negative intentions to transmute their energies into positive, higher divine channels of energy. Michael is usually invoked as a champion against adversity, to increase courage and positive outcomes. I often use the affirmation of the archangel St. Michael. For protection in any situation, repeat three times: "Divine light of the highest order, under the protection of the archangel St. Michael." This affirmation can be of great comfort and promote a sense of peace in unsettling situations.

Michael is also the guiding light of our particular historical epoch. In *The Many Faces of Angels,* Harvey Humann explains it this way: "Michael has a special mission to perform in the earth, to bring down to human levels a better understanding of the meaning of peace, beauty and love. He is a spiritual force working from invisible planes to awaken within us the Christ consciousness that is implanted in every soul." Michael impulses are guiding people toward the awareness of the spiritual world and the ability to tame the dragon of materialistic thinking and evil intentions. Michael sends impulses into the souls of individual human beings to open their minds to new ways of thinking and to instill the courage to figure our spiritual experiences out for ourselves. Michael's guidance integrates well with free will.

Like all angels, Michael waits until we are ready to face his light of transformation. All this talk about breaking molds and old ways of thinking has a basis in the essence of Michael's influence. In *Angels and Mortals,* James H. Hindes beautifully states: "An idea sent by Michael is characterized by the life it awakens in our hearts and will. Michaelic thoughts are not abstract but want to be felt, willed and ultimately, 'real-ized' on earth; for a spiritual idea when thought by a human being on earth, when grasped in the mind as an ideal, has the power to elevate something earthly into higher realms."

Humans exist in two worlds, the physical and the spiritual. In the past, humans have thought of life on earth only in terms of its physical aspect. Now, in many exciting and creative ways, humans are integrating their physical experience with their spiritual experience. Many avenues to the spiritual world exist because we are finding our own ways based on our own paths of creativity and love. If your spiritual quests and paths are expanding, this means you have consciously or unconsciously turned toward the light of Michael. If not, now is the time to do so, especially if you choose to be an angel warrior committed to lightening up the world. I guarantee that you will be hearing more and more about this special archangel in the days to come. Michael's name means "Who Is God?" This is a question we are all asking in our own ways, and the answers are setting us free.

RAPHAEL
(FROM THE HEBREW *RAPHA',* WHICH MEANS
"TO HEAL," AND *'EL,* WHICH MEANS "GOD")

Raphael's name means "God Has Healed." Raphael is charged with the healing of the earth and the humans who live on the earth. Raphael is also the guardian and treasurer of creative talents. Healers and artists who bring beauty to the earth are under the influence of Raphael. Beauty is healing to the soul; it is a way the angels promote healing. When we behold a beautiful scene in nature or a magnificent work of art, we can be healed if we learn how to channel the energy of beauty directly to our soul and spirit. Many healers are discovering that in order to practice the healing arts in the most effective holistic way, they must create a space of beauty for their healing energy. This is done by incorporating sound and music, fragrance, healing colors, and art, and by clearing the area of negative influences by bringing in the light of the healing angels, who are under the mastery of Raphael. Raphael's energy is transformative; it heals the soul of despair and depression, filling the space with self-love and virtues and bringing balance.

GABRIEL
(FROM THE HEBREW *GEBHER*, WHICH MEANS "MAN," AND *EL*, WHICH MEANS "GOD")

Gabriel is associated with a trumpet, symbolizing the voice of God. Gabriel is a bringer of good news and a maker of changes. Gabriel has been credited with announcing the birth of Christ to Mary; with being the guardian of the prophet Muhammad in the Muslim tradition; with being the angel who inspired Joan of Arc to help the king of France; and with influencing Zoroaster. Gabriel announces to qualified humans the major duties of their spiritual commission for the benefit of the earth. If Gabriel has not spoken or appeared to you to clarify your spiritual gifts, try tuning into his essence. Gabriel has many angels under his influence whom we can tune into for guidance and messages regarding the special part we play in the big picture. So allow messages to come through to inspire you; you may even hear the faint or blasting sound of a trumpet as you receive your messages from God.

URIEL
(FROM THE HEBREW, MEANING "FIRE OF GOD")

Uriel is an angel of prophecy who imparts transforming ideas to humans for the realization of goals. The angels under the guidance of Uriel are alchemists who can transform the discouraged and weak, and set them back on their path of love. Uriel is also associated with arts such as music and literature. Uriel's fire inspires teachers, and brings life to ideas. Uriel is also the archangel to call on in spiritual emergencies; in true spiritual emergencies, the angels of Uriel restore salvation and sanity. In other words, when you get too far away from your center, call out to Uriel.

HANIEL
("GLORY OR GRACE OF GOD")

Haniel is said to be the governor of Venus. Venus, as you know, is the planet of love and pleasure. It rules over our capacity to express affectionate love and to enjoy beauty. Venus also inspires social grace, harmony, and friendship between humans. Haniel is the angel who inspires all powers of love and can also be invoked as a power against evil. Haniel can bestow happiness and make life more beautiful. The human experience is so special when we have love and happiness from within. The angels of Haniel will make sure our angel warriorship has the fun and warmth of being human in a beautiful world. In your meditations, ask to visit the planet Venus and imagine meeting its governor, Haniel. It is a planet of pink light with metallic flecks reflecting colored light—beautiful colors we don't experience on earth. Bring some of this light back to earth with you; it will increase beauty and happiness around you.

RAZIEL
("SECRET OF GOD")

Raziel is the archangel of the mysteries. We encounter certain mysteries during our search for spiritual truth. Raziel is the guardian of originality and knowledge. Raziel is said to live in the habitat Chokmah, the realm of pure ideas. The angels under the guidance of Raziel can be thought of as muses who inspire us with original ideas and pure thoughts of knowledge. What we do with this knowledge and inspiration is part of the unfolding mystery, part of the larger plan for the earth.

AURIEL

Auriel is the angel of night and winter. Auriel is associated with the creative earth energy of winter, the ebb period when the seed is in the earth and all is dark. Auriel is the angel of our future selves; he helps us contemplate the future. Auriel watches over humans in the germinating stage of ideas and thoughts and brings practicality and earth energy to them for creation. When you are in an ebb period of your life, creating a new future, call upon the angels of Auriel for guidance.

ANGEL HIERARCHIES

I am just beginning to understand the hierarchies of angels and archangels. The Theosophists have many explicit and interesting books concerning the unseen world of angel hierarchy and order. A lot of angel warriors just don't have the time to spend studying these ideas because they are involved in their human missions. To my mind, the mission is more important than getting caught up in wordy details. Just keep in mind that there is a time for study and a time for action, both of which we must personally balance in our lives. Know that order among angels exists, but also know that you are guided by a higher power; you don't need to know all the exact details to receive the benefits. Imagine the archangels in whatever way works for you; they are there for you, waiting to guide your natural energies.

Practice 1: Living the Prayer of St. Francis

A Prayer of Saint Francis of Assisi

Lord, make me an instrument of Your peace.
Where there is hatred, let me sow love.
Where there is injury, pardon,

Where there is doubt, faith
Where there is despair, hope,
Where there is darkness, light,
    and where there is sadness, joy.

O Divine Master, grant that I may not so much
    seek to be consoled, as to console;
To be understood, as to understand;
To be loved, as to love;
For it is in giving that we receive –
It is in pardoning that we are pardoned;
And it is in dying that we are born to eternal
    life.

This prayer offers a guideline to angel warriorship. Read it, meditate on it, and sense how you resonate with it. We cannot fully live by these ideas unless we are centered in the abundance qualities of the angels. When we become an instrument of peace and give hope, faith, light, and love, we ourselves will never run out of these qualities; they will increase in strength around us. When they are given freely and unconditionally, these qualities multiply, sending beams of angelic energy throughout the universe.

Practice 2: Kindness and Compassion

Whether one believes in a religion or not, and whether one believes in rebirth or not, there isn't anyone who doesn't appreciate kindness and compassion.

The Dalai Lama

True compassion is never effortful or forced, and it is not planned. It is a response shown by people who are *freely* able to show kindness and love to all creation. Compassion happens spontaneously when we realize the connectedness of all life, internalizing the fact that regardless of differences in culture, philosophy, and race, human beings are all the same. If we took our skin off, we would basically look the same. The driving life force within us is to be happy and avoid suffering; we share this with all humans. An angel warrior must get in touch with the true essence of kindness and compassion. Angel warriors must adopt a policy of kindness to follow in their own lives. This requires wisdom and knowing exactly what kindness is. We may need to change or expand our own ideas about kindness. Some of us may think we are being kind when we give materially or when we do things for people. We must look deep into our hearts when we give; sometimes it is kinder not to give. Kindness and compassion are not intellectual; they require human action out in the world. The right intentions and spiritual beliefs are not worth a lot until they are taken out into the world. True kindness and compassion can transform the darkness of despair in whomever they touch. A little kindness goes a long way. It allows a positive field of love to progress into infinity. Who could trade the feeling we get when we show kindness and compassion to others? It is truly beyond compare.

Practice 3: Angels in Training and Angels on Call

Something fun and exciting happening in the collective unconscious is the idea of "angels in training." Each time I have done an angel workshop, some of the participants have identified themselves as angels in training. I first came across this idea from a group of very special women, who refer to themselves as the A.I.T.s; amazing angel happenings take place around them every day. This is a wonderful idea for our spiritual path, and anyone can play. Our paths are all unique, and we can incorporate the idea of being in training for angelhood in our own ways. If you decide to become an angel in training, be ready for some awe-inspiring angel events to take place in your life.

Another fun idea my friend Jai and her son Brandon came up with is "angels on call." They found that when they designated times to be "on call," situations would arise in which they would be at the right place at the right time to be of great assistance to someone. You may be an angel on call and not even realize it. The angels know just when to summon you. If you are involved in something else at the time and are not readily available, they will call someone else. You can think of being on call as being part of the angelic reserve for earthly duty. The angels reward you by keeping you safe, bringing humor to your life, and giving you that wonderful, warm feeling that comes when we really help others and bring them hope. Being on call can mean sending out light to others and staying aware of and attuned to your own light. You can send your light out to others whenever you get the urge. As you drive by people on the street who look sad, send them some angels. If I'm driving by a car accident and human help has already arrived, I send angels to join the effort by asking my guardian angel to send extra light to the situation.

You can come up with ideas like this, and the angels will play right along with you. Focusing on your angel cheerleaders is also fun. It is important to bring good cheer to others; it will lighten them up. Just being cheerful and happy is a way in itself of giving people around you an angel experience. So have fun, remember to stay light, and always give from a center of angelic abundance.

Practice 4: The Power of Prayer and Intercession

I want to stress again the power of prayer and intercession. I've talked about blessing others and sending out light to them, which are prayer techniques, and now I would like to offer other prayer ideas. Prayer is of great importance for deepening our spiritual strength. Many people pray every day. Prayer is between ourselves and our higher power; in other words, it is personal. I know almost all of us either pray consistently or pray when we feel compelled. Prayer is a powerful, divine intercession tactic.

You can turn every thought you have into a prayer by calling on the higher power and the angels. When you send out a letter, send a prayer with it. Also do this when you make a phone call. You can go through your day in an almost constant state of prayer, a constant communication with the angels. This goes on at a higher level, and we may not even be conscious of it. If you want to be more conscious of it, just be more aware of how you communicate with your higher power.

Many people have angel prayer groups and angel healing groups that meet regularly. Dorie D'Angelo, who wrote the book *Living With Angels*, started a healing group many years ago. She joined the angels in 1984, but the group still meets regularly and her husband André keeps it going. A chapter in her book gives good guidance if you want to start an angel healing group or if you are already participating in one. When people get together to share angel experiences and help others through prayer and communication, angel happenings take on a new meaning. We need each other, and meeting with the angels in mind helps us learn more about who we are and how we can be of higher service.

Chapter 18

"Don't Give Up; We Like Who You Are!"

I started this book a year ago. Throughout this year, the changels (angels of change) have been very active in my life. Situations arose that I never could have imagined would ever take place. It seems as though somewhere at some time I asked the angels to lift the veils hiding all the illusions that I was attached to. And it's not over yet! It's just amazing all the large and small lessons I go through each day and sometimes each moment when I am truly awake. I meet many people and I ask if they have noticed major shifts in their lives; invariably, they say yes and share a few of these happenings with me.

I also hear all sorts of explanations for these shifts. I don't think that these shifts relate simply to the alignment of planets or to eclipses, and so forth, although these elements could have an influence on us. Mainly, I observe that things have gotten out of control on the planet as a whole. Overcrowding, overspending, overpolluting, and so forth are now at the point where we can no longer ignore the problems of Mother Earth and the humans that inhabit her. Look into any corner of our communal existence (education, the economy, housing, health, and welfare), and you will find a serious and usually outrageous blunder and injustice. No matter how hard we try to hide from the problems of existence, sooner or later we have to confront ourselves and the situations around us. And the sooner, the better.

Right now, positive thinking and hope are of the utmost importance. Again I will address the argument that hope is not good because it keeps us from "living fully in the moment" and focuses on the future. Well, that is the very point! Live in the now, but nourish hope for the future. If you're feeling that the world around you is crashing in, you're not alone, and it is all the more essential to cultivate hope. The angels are our hope gardeners.

Many of you have invited the angels to journey with you on your spiritual path. The lessons don't necessarily get easier when we bring along the angels, and quite often they can be intense. This is one of the angels' greatest gifts. When we make it through these lessons and obstacles, we learn how the angels are guiding us and that we must not give up. When we reach our darkest hour, it may seem as though the angels have abandoned us. This could not be farther from the truth. At such times, the angels are not external; they are dwelling inside you at the very heart of your soul. If we look outside of ourselves in our darkest moments, sometimes we may miss the light. Look inside; I promise the light is there. If you find yourself lost in the darkness, just hold on for that "one more moment," and the light will flood in. The angels' love is constant. God's love is constant. Trust and keep the faith; don't abandon the positive principles you strive to live by at the very moment you truly need them. Pray, and ask the angels to keep you safe. Hang in there; no matter what, you will be okay. To quote a foremost authority on the subject of spiritual dilemmas, St. Teresa of Avila, "Let nothing disturb you, let nothing frighten you: everything passes away except God. God alone suffices."

Angel Cheerleaders

Remember to listen for the voices of the angel cheerleaders.
They are cheering us around the clock to be our personal best.
Listen closely and you will hear cheers from your angel cheerleaders, similar to the following: "Don't give up; we like who are
you! You are not alone; God loves you unconditionally, and so
do we! Go for it [your goals]; listen to your heart! You deserve
to be happy; you have everything it takes! There is a beautiful
heavenly love light at the end of the tunnel! You are light! Everything is going to be okay! Know it! Pray."

Go into angel alpha state and start to visualize the angels cheering. Pretty soon, they will come into view on the screen of your
imagination. You will start to feel all warm and glowing and you'll
get the urge to smile, sing, or join in with their cheers. You also
may get the uncontrollable desire to laugh, because there is an
aspect of humor in every human's life, especially when viewed
from on high. Have a good laugh; it is very healing.

Keep your mind full of the angels and their messages of light
and hope, and you will learn how to live in peace and harmony
with every step you take. If you are wondering what I am like
or who I am, I have only one request: Do not confuse the finger
that is pointing at the moon with the moon.

I wish all of you the happiness that resides in your cells and
tickles your funny bone, a flock of angel blessings, and an aura
of mental peace that clings to your very soul.

Recommended Reading

I want to take this time to recommend a few books I have read
this year that helped me through my personal changes and that
answered many of my questions. These books arrived on the
scene just when I needed them most.

Morning Has Been All Night Coming (New York: Berkeley/
Putnum, 1991) by John Harricharan is full of wisdom, fun to

read, and inspiring; it bestows a pragmatic approach to the mystical and sacred. The end result is that we realize we can live *in* this world as effective teachers to all, but not be *of* the world. Don't forget to read his first book, *When You Can Walk on Water Take the Boat* (New York: Berkely/Putnum, 1990). If you read either one of John's books, you will end up with a feeling of pure hope and an "incredible lightness of being."

Dan Millman's new book, *Sacred Journey of the Peaceful Warrior* (Tiburon, CA: HJ Kramer, 1991), is incredible. All I can say is that I am awestruck by this book and probably will be for a very long time.

Thich Nhat Hanh's *Peace Is Every Step: The Path of Mindfulness in Everyday Life* (New York: Bantam, 1991) is full of wonderful practices to bring peace, serenity, and beauty to your everyday life. Take your angels along when you read this book, and you'll have a winning combination.

Chapter 19

Angel Extras

Angelic Formulas

This section contains philosophical thoughts and formulas I have found to be helpful in the quest for attracting angels and developing angel mindfulness.

★

Be authentic, be yourself naturally, and you will know your higher purpose.

★

Your attitude and reaction to life can make either heaven or hell on earth.

★

Discover God, a higher power, in your own way, and express yourself as a gift of God, an authentic being of love.

★

To attract, be attractive.

★

What you give up, you win; the thing that binds you is the thing that frees you.

★

To thine own self be true. Beware of misplaced sympathy. Give to yourself first to create an abundance to automatically share with the world.

★

Mentally relax, take yourself lightly, and don't concern yourself with problems and worries. The key to creativity is to "undisturb" yourself. This is also the best way to tune into the angels' realm for messages of inspiration.

★

Leave yourself alone. Don't think so much. Go outside of yourself. Stop analyzing every little thing you do.

★

Allow other people to just be – whoever, whatever, whenever. Be a "permissionary." Defining and labeling others will limit the view you have of yourself.

★

No one is a failure who has friends.

★

Know where you are going, and don't be afraid to take your time getting there. What's the hurry?

★

Character is destiny; if you change your character, you
change what happens to you. Free will entitles us to create
our own fate and luck.

★

Optimism is your best defense against attacks or criticism from
other people. You are free to perceive other people's intentions
however you want: If you treat them as if they are positive
toward you, regardless of their actions, attacks will dissolve.

★

You may not like the behavior and actions of others, but
to label them bad is to take away possibilities for change.
Anytime you want to call or label a person something
negative, rephrase and say to yourself, This person is
temporarily acting like "something negative."

★

Whatever you fear the most, you may well create or attract.
Fear is negative power.

★

Allow a state of divine indifference to operate around you. Go
with the flow; let things happen instead of making them
happen.

★

Friction brings fatigue.

★

Surrender to win.

★

Cease expecting, and you gain all things.

★

Basic human problems such as fear, suffering, and tension are *not* relieved by the material comforts created by science and technology, but by the development of personal spiritual values.

★

We are spiritual beings having a human experience.

Guided Meditation: Angel Innocence

This is a guided meditation of a spiritual nature. You will automatically receive other benefits, but it is designed to raise your spiritual vibration so that you can program yourself for positive experiences. Read through the meditation first, then try it. You can read a portion, then meditate on it. You may want to tape-record a version and add music and other elements, such as relaxation techniques, that help you meditate. Use the meditation suggestions as a guideline and add in what you want, as if you were using a recipe and slightly modifying the ingredients.

Allow yourself at least fifteen to twenty minutes of peaceful time to receive any real benefits, even if you just sit still for fifteen minutes and nothing "exciting" happens. The benefits will show up later in some way. The main attitude of this meditation is angel innocence (nonjudgment). Innocence is within each of us; it resides at the core of our being. Getting in touch with your innocence, or reuniting with it, will bring you increased happiness and optimism. This may be the beginning step for uncovering your true essence — your special light color, waiting to shine clear and bright to transform the world around you. If you feel silly at any time during this exercise and get the urge to giggle, go ahead. This is a sure sign that the angels are near! Remember to take this lightly — no seriousness please.

★

Sit comfortably. If you lie down, you may fall asleep. Falling asleep is okay, but first try it sitting. Go into angel alpha state. Take a deep breath into your abdomen, then exhale, relaxing your body. When you feel relaxed and physically comfortable, notice the change in sounds you hear and the change in your level of awareness. Start to focus on the electrical center of your brain.

Allow a warm flood of golden pink light to glow at this center. The light calms you and you begin to feel the loving protection of your angels as the light glows brighter. Electrical impulses — your brain waves — begin to slow their speed. Use your imagination to visualize the waves slowing to a gentle rolling rhythm. Establish mental peace. You may begin to have thoughts. Thoughts will leave peacefully when no meaning is attached to them. Keep in mind, in your peaceful mind, that thought knows nothing of love; love is from the heart. Don't force thoughts away. If one disturbing thought seems to stay, mentally release it by not reacting. Ask the angels to take the thought away and transmute it.

Imagine yourself in the realm of the angels, where there is no gravity. Visualize your thoughts orbiting by, coming close, then spinning off. If you find yourself concentrating, stop. If you find you are contemplating, stop. Pay attention to attention, without using effort.

Begin to surround yourself in white light that glitters with flecks of pink and gold; feel how the flecks mingle with your own cells and bring you peace. Begin to focus on the innocence of a young child. This young child is you. If a negative thought is competing for attention, ask the angels for an eraser and erase it from your consciousness. Visualize this child, and tell the child he or she is loved and protected by angels and is one with a guardian angel at all times. Let your innocence expand. Whatever happens now, view it through the soul window of your innocent child. Visualize a flower and its fragrance; see it with the wonder of a child. Flowers are the art projects of angels. Imagine yourself running through a field of flowers. The flowers reach out to you and softly brush you with more innocence as you glide by them.

Know that this child is your higher self. The spirit of wisdom has filled your being. You are one with the protected child. Now you are with the angels—innocent and loved—yet filled with infinite wisdom. You have raised your vibration by opening your mind as an innocent child. Your angelic energy system is now fully intact. There are messages and seeds of ideas for the angels to plant. So, be still, don't judge, don't look for the sensational, and stay with the love. Messages will become thoughts at some time, usually later when you don't expect them. It is important to stay in the center of the mental peace you have created; if you leave this space, come back in. This is a time for inner preparation and cultivation; it is not a time for activity. It is a time of quiet education about your inner self.

Up to this point, you have allowed some inner education time. It is now time to program and deprogram your mind if you want to. Ask the angels to help you affirm the positive. If something negative bubbles in, be objective. If it says you are not worthy or causes anger, stand apart from your emotional self—don't react. Use awareness as an eraser and erase the negative emotion and replace the space with joy. Program positive thoughts and affirmations that will stay with you, replacing any negative programs or thoughts. Do this in whatever way works for you. You can make declarations and ask the angels to bless your goals and aspirations. Allow some time for this process; then, when you are finished, begin to change your awareness to the beta level of awakeness.

Before you reenter earth's atmosphere, take a moment to release all mental gravity from your face. Allow a radiant, peaceful smile to begin expanding until it flows throughout your body. Tension is leaving your facial muscles, and your eyes feel bright and clear; you are now looking at the world through a heavenly rose crystal glass, and your senses are attuned to divine humor and bliss. Listen to the giggles and twinkling laughter of the angels; resonate with the vibration of their joy. Take a deep breath and allow joy to permeate your cells. Now come back gently and slowly. Remain with the bliss; remain centered; remain in the joy of divine humor.

When your consciousness is awake and ready to face the stimulus of the world around you, move around and stretch if you like. Know that you are now a lighter being, and your light will be reflected in everything you do.

★

More Innocence: A Note From Elizabeth Ann Godfrey (Ten Years Old)

Angels are very special. They love to help you if you are having troubles. Angels will tell you to do the right thing. They are very beautiful and do things for God. They tell you in your heart to be good.

Angels are everywhere. You have a guardian angel. Your guardian angel loves you very much, and so do the rest of the angels. Angels are messengers of God and do whatever he says. Some of the things he probably tells angels to do is stop someone from being bad.

Angels guide you when you are sleeping and when you are awake. They are always with you. You can't get away from them even if you hide — they are still there. They are magical, at least that is what I think.

Interview With Jessica Marie Godfrey (Six Years Old)

Q) *Where is heaven?*
A) [She points up to the sky.]

Q) *Who lives in heaven?*
A) God, Jesus, Mary, St. Joseph, the saints, people that died that lived down here, good people are in the main heaven,

like me. Robbers go to the other place in heaven made for robbers, a bad part of heaven.

Q) *What goes on in the bad part?*
A) Bad people fight.

Q) *What are angels?*
A) People that are very good. They fly and are a little more specialer than us, like an inch farther away.

Q) *Do we see them?*
A) No.

Q) *How do we know what they are like if we don't see them?*
A) Well, there is pictures of them, and statues, cards like them.

Q) *How do we know angels are around us?*
A) Because they love us like God loves us and we have a guardian angel. I can see the flames of them, not quite their wings, but their bodies. See the little dots in the air, that is the angels I think.

Glossary and Angel Resources

ANGEL® Cards: You can order or buy ANGEL® cards at most "New Consciousness" bookstores. They are also included in "The Game of Transformation." Both the cards and the game can be ordered by contacting:

> Music Design
> 1845 N. Farwell Ave.
> Milwaukee, WI 53202
> 1-800-862-7232

Retail or wholesale orders are accepted. (The ANGEL® cards are now available in French, German, and Spanish as well as English.)

Changels: The angels of change and transformation. They are everywhere these days!

Guardian Angel Prayer Card: You can find these in Catholic bookstores and religious supply stores.

Permissionaries: People who allow change in their own thinking and changes in others, no matter how absurd or crazy it all may seem.

Works Cited Bibliography

In the interest of maintaining the tone of this book, I did not want to weigh you down with extensive footnotes in the text. This bibliography will enable you to track down the sources for most of the quotations cited in the text.

Chesterton, G. K. *Orthodoxy*. Garden City, NY: Image, 1959, p. 120.

Chopra, Deepak. *Quantum Healing*. New York, NY: Bantam, 1989, p. 88.

Church, F. Forrester. *Entertaining Angels: A Guide to Heaven for Atheists and True Believers*. San Francisco: Harper and Row, 1987, p. 27.

Cousens, Ken. *Look Upon the Children*. Self-Published, 1986.

Dalai Lama. *A Policy of Kindness*, Sidney Piburn (Ed.). Ithaca, NY: Snow Lion Publications, 1990, pp. 56 and 52.

D'Angelo, Dorie. *Living With Angels*. Carmel, CA: First Church of Angels, 1980, p. 109.

Fields, Rick. *Chop Wood, Carry Water*. Los Angeles: Jeremy P. Tarcher, 1984, p. 5.

Hindes, James H. In *Angels and Mortals: Their Co-Creative Powers*, Maria Parisen (Ed.). Wheaton, IL: Quest Books, 1990, p. 122.

Humann, Harvey. *The Many Faces of Angels*. Marina del Rey, CA: DeVorss and Co., 1986, p. 68.

James, William. Cited in Norman Vincent Peale, *My Favorite Quotations*. New York, NY: Harper and Row, 1990, p. 94.

Jeffrey, Francis. Cited in Terry Taylor, *Messengers of Light*. Tiburon, CA: HJ Kramer, 1990, p. 174.

Klein, Allen. *The Healing Power of Humor*. Los Angeles: Jeremy P. Tarcher, 1990, p. 95.

Kübler-Ross, Elisabeth. "Death Does Not Exist." Cited in Bauman et al., *The Holistic Health Handbook*. Berkeley, CA: And/Or Press, 1978, p. 439.

Long-Chen-Pa. Cited in Barry Stevens, *Burst Out Laughing*. Berkeley, CA: Celestial Arts, 1984, p. 177.

Maclean, Dorothy. *To Hear the Angels Sing*. Issaquah, WA: Lorian Press, 1987, pp. 148, 21, and 187.

May, Rollo. *The Courage to Create*. New York, NY: Bantam, 1980, p. 4.

Newhouse, Flower A. *Rediscovering the Angels*. Escondido, CA: The Christwatch Ministry, 1976, p. 60.

Newton, John. "Amazing Grace." Cited in John Bartlett (Ed.), *Bartlett's Quotations*. Boston: Little, Brown and Co., 1955.

Peale, Norman Vincent. *My Favorite Quotations*. New York, NY: Harper and Row, 1990, p. 36.

Peale, Norman Vincent. *The Power of Positive Thinking*. New York, NY: Prentice-Hall, 1952.

Peale, Norman Vincent. *The Tough Minded Optimist*. Englewood Cliffs, NJ: Prentice Hall, 1961, p. 127.

Peck, M. Scott. *People of the Lie*. New York, NY: Simon and Schuster, 1983, p. 264.

Peck, M. Scott. *The Road Less Traveled*. New York, NY: Simon and Schuster, 1978, pp. 266, 238.

Roman, Sanaya. *Spiritual Growth*. Tiburon, CA: HJ Kramer, 1989, p. 18.

Ronner, John. *Do You Have a Guardian Angel?* Idialantic, FL: Mamre Press, 1985, p. 137.

Siegel, Bernie. In *Healers on Healing*, Richard Carlson and Benjamin Shields (Eds.). Los Angeles: Jeremy P. Tarcher, 1989, p. 7.

Spinoza, Baruch. Cited in Norman Vincent Peale, *My Favorite Quotations*. New York, NY: Harper and Row, 1990, p. 66.

St. Teresa of Avila. "Oh my Lord!" Cited in Leonard Foley (Ed.), *Saint of the Day*. Cincinnati, OH: St. Anthony Messenger Press, 1975, p. 116.

Trevelyan, Sir George. From the foreword to *Talking With Nature* by Michael J. Roads. Tiburon, CA: HJ Kramer, 1987, p. 11.

Trungpa, Chogyam. In *Challenge of the Heart*, John Welwood (Ed.). Boston: Shambhala Publications, Inc., 1985, p. 59.

Trungpa, Chogyam. *Shambhala, The Sacred Path of the Warrior*. New York, NY: Bantam, 1986, p. 8.

Dear Reader:

Terry Taylor is collecting angel stories, angel artists, and angel poets for her *Angel Newsletter*.

Please write if you would like to be included on her mailing list for the newsletter or for the angel workshops and seminars she offers. If you would like to schedule a workshop or angel talk in your town, or have an angel conference/consultation, please write for details.

If you are interested in tapes of workshops and other angel topics, please write.

Terry Taylor
Angels Can Fly
2275 Huntington Drive #326
San Marino, CA 91108

COMPATIBLE BOOKS

FROM H J KRAMER INC

MESSENGERS OF LIGHT:
THE ANGELS' GUIDE TO SPIRITUAL GROWTH
by Terry Lynn Taylor
At last, a practical way to connect with the
angels and to bring heaven into your life!

ANSWERS FROM THE ANGELS:
A BOOK OF ANGEL LETTERS
by Terry Lynn Taylor
Terry shares the letters she has received from people
all over the world that tell of their experiences with angels.

CREATING WITH THE ANGELS
by Terry Lynn Taylor
A journey into creativity, including powerful
exercises and assistance from the angels.

WAY OF THE PEACEFUL WARRIOR
by Dan Millman
A tale of transformation and adventure . . .
a worldwide best-seller.

SACRED JOURNEY OF THE PEACEFUL WARRIOR
by Dan Millman
"After you've read SACRED JOURNEY, you will know
what possibilities await you." — WHOLE LIFE TIMES

NO ORDINARY MOMENTS
by Dan Millman
Based on the premise that we can change our world by
changing ourselves, Dan shares an approach to life that turns
obstacles into opportunities, and experiences into wisdom.

THE LIFE YOU WERE BORN TO LIVE:
A GUIDE TO FINDING YOUR LIFE PURPOSE
by Dan Millman
A modern method based on ancient wisdom that can help
you find new meaning, purpose, and direction in your life.

TALKING WITH NATURE
by Michael J. Roads
"From Australia comes a major new writer . . . a magnificent book!"
— RICHARD BACH, Author, *Jonathan Livingston Seagull*

JOURNEY INTO NATURE
by Michael J. Roads
"If you only read one book this year, make that book
JOURNEY INTO NATURE." — FRIEND'S REVIEW

COMPATIBLE BOOKS

FROM H J KRAMER INC

THE EARTH LIFE SERIES
by Sanaya Roman
*A course in learning to live with joy,
sense energy, and grow spiritually.*

LIVING WITH JOY, BOOK I
*"I like this book because it describes the way I feel
about so many things."* — VIRGINIA SATIR

PERSONAL POWER THROUGH AWARENESS:
A GUIDEBOOK FOR SENSITIVE PEOPLE, BOOK II
"Every sentence contains a pearl. . . ." — LILIAS FOLAN

SPIRITUAL GROWTH:
BEING YOUR HIGHER SELF, BOOK III
*Orin teaches how to reach upward to align with the
higher energies of the universe, look inward to expand
awareness, and move outward in world service.*

An Orin/DaBen Book
CREATING MONEY
by Sanaya Roman and Duane Packer, Ph.D.
This best-selling book teaches advanced manifesting techniques.

BRIDGE OF LIGHT
by LaUna Huffines
Tools of light for spiritual transformation — a spiritual classic.

SON-RISE: THE MIRACLE CONTINUES
by Barry Neil Kaufman
*The inspiring true story of one family's triumph over helplessness
that started a revolution of love for autistic and other special children.*

UNDERSTAND YOUR DREAMS
by Alice Anne Parker
*A practical book that offers the reader
the key to dream interpretation.*

THE WIZDOM WITHIN
by Susan Jean and Dr. Irving Oyle
*"Fascinating! Illuminating. . . .
Reading this book can be hazardous to your preconceptions."*
— WILLIS HARMON, President, Institute of Noetic Sciences